From Darkness to Sunshine
A Young Boy's Odyssey

Twentieth Century Miracle

by

Mark Bernard Kupfer

Edited by

Debby R. Kupfer

Illustrations by

Hugo Marquez

DORRANCE PUBLISHING CO., INC.
PITTSBURGH, PENNSYLVANIA 15222

ISBN # 0-8059-5827-4

Printed in the United States of America

First Printing
For information or to order additional books, please write:
Dorrance Publishing Co., Inc.
643 Smithfield Street
Pittsburgh, Pennsylvania 15222
U.S.A.
1-800-788-7654
Or visit our web site and on-line catalog at www.dorrancepublishing.com

Dedication

This narrative was not written with ink; it was written with my tears and blood. Through my own personal grief, I can see the faces of six million innocent Jewish people brutally murdered in gas chambers and in countless other ways. I dedicate this work to my beloved parents and family members who perished in the Holocaust.

Father:	Dov (Berek) Kupfer	Mother:	Devorah Kupfer
Brothers:	Moses	Sisters:	Zeitel
	Peretz		Luba
	Israel		Chana

Holocaust Survivors:
Harry (deceased)
Mayer (Mark, myself) (deceased December 7, 1998)
Sarah

It gives us great pride and honor to proclaim the dedication of this book to our father, tate, friend, and abbah, Mark B. Kupfer. May his words that he wrote be a lesson to all that we must never forget about the atrocities of Hitler so that they will never happen again. Our father taught us that we must never be afraid of who we are or where we came from.

Unfortunately, our father passed away before he could see the publication of this book. With love, his children Dov Emil, Debby Rene, Samuel Paul, and Abie Jack.

To my father with love and dedication;
your life's goal is now a reality.

Debby R. Kupfer
Editor

Contents

Introduction

Most of this narrative relates to my childhood years in Poland. All the stories that follow, which I can never forget, actually happened. I saw with my own eyes the terrible brutality that happened to the Jews of Europe, not only to my family, but also to friends, neighbors, and innocent children.

I am a Holocaust survivor. You will discover through my story what it was like to be Jewish in the years 1933 to 1945. But I will also take you through the journey of my entire life, from being an innocent child growing up in the treacherous time of the Holocaust in Europe, to my life in the United States.

CHAPTER I

From Darkness to Sunshine:
A Young Boy's Odyssey

In the days before yellow Stars of David appeared in Poland, life was good in my native town, Nowy Korczyn. It is in the heart of the country between two major rivers, the Wisla and the Nida. The Wisla is the longest Polish river, rising in the Carpathian Mountains near the Czechoslovakia border and flowing north into the Baltic Sea. The Nida is a tributary of the Wilsa that surrounded the town and was lined with beautiful trees and bushes. It was also used as a highway for commerce entering the town.

Poland was the largest country in Central Europe, with a population of 35 million, three million of whom were Jews. In my country of birth, the seasons of the year were easily distinguished. In the spring, the buds and the grass were green and one could smell the freshness of the new growth. The townspeople showed love for the land by working outdoors, either on their farms and in their gardens. The summer offered other enjoyments. We went to the segregated beaches, one for men and one for women. The parks were full of activity; children played ball, rode homemade bicycles, and played various games. My father rented a cottage in the country, and we stayed there on weekends.

In the fall, when leaves fell from the trees, we collected them to be burned in the stove, providing warmth in the winter. There was abundant rain and often hail, a sign that the days were getting shorter. When winter came, there was very little sun and an enormous amount of snow. There were days when we missed school because of the heavy snowfall. We had warm clothing for winter, and the entertainment included sledding and ice skating. Indoors, we children listened to Jewish music, stories, and prayers. The farmers came to buy merchandise and took their

1

purchases back to the farm on horse-drawn sleighs. The inhabitants of the town were educators, business people, shoemakers, tailors, and storekeepers.

I, Mark Bernard Kupfer, born November 18, 1929, was the second youngest of nine children, five boys and four girls. My father's name was Dov, or Berek in Polish. My mother Devorah, was named for the biblical prophetess, the freedom fighter of Hebrew history—the Jewish Joan of Arc. She was devoted to her family, charitable with her neighbors; yet a businesswoman too, who raised her children according to Jewish laws and traditions. She was known as the "queen of the city." My mother had a round rosy face with big blue eyes. She wore a wig most of the time, since it was a customary for a Jewish woman to shave off her hair after marriage.

For generations the Kupfers were respected citizens, and our name was well known to businessmen throughout Poland. My father was a prominent Jewish resident of the town. He had blue eyes and a long beard and was a very religious man. Learned in Jewish law, he was known in Hebrew as a Dayan, a Judge who advised people in matters of right and wrong. He was a wealthy, dignified, and knowledgeable businessman. As a member of the City Council, he was admired for his efforts to make the community a haven for Jews.

Our family owned two stores and a wholesale house. One store sold dry goods and the other was a drugstore where only medicine was sold. The wholesale house dealt in sugar, salt, and ceramic oven tiles. My sister Tzeitel, a pharmacist, managed the drugstore with the help of a male pharmacist of German descent.

Let me describe for you the years from 1933 to 1938. In 1933, when I was about four, a man named Adolf Hitler came to power in Germany. How could that affect us, living safely hundreds of miles away in Poland? What could he do to the Jews even in Germany, where they held considerable power as owners of railroads, stores, and banks, and were important contributors to the German economy?

The name Hitler meant nothing to me because I was reaching an important and longed-for stage of my childhood. I entered Cheder to study Hebrew, the Five Books of Moses, and, eventually the commentaries of Rashi, the great eleventh-century scholar who expounded on the Talmud. I was proud because someday I would understand the Talmud, the basis of Jewish laws and lore. I was far more concerned about what we would eat for our noontime meal than about Hitler! Would it be a good nourishing soup that my mother knew so well how to prepare or maybe potatoes and bread and perhaps today a piece of meat? I thought about the kind of hat my mother would let me pick out at the market down the street. Should it be the broad brimmed hat favored along the checkered border, a cap, or perhaps the round, flat-topped one with a little visor that so many students wore? Should I run out to play with my friend Solomon, to whom I could brag about learning to read Hebrew on the cobbled street of Kvalewski Ulica?

Perhaps I might just sit on the doorstep of the store. Beyond this was the kitchen, and farther on was the living room where the beds and table were the major pieces of furniture. On the doorstep I could watch the Polish housewives hurrying to

2

market for their daily purchases. We lacked refrigerators at the time, so we stored food in the cold cellar. I watched the porters amble by, drawing their carts behind them or pushing heavy ones with a long shaft. The fortunate richer ones used horses to pull the wooden carts. These carts had fared sides that could bear people, produce, or merchandise. Automobiles were a rarity. Most of the people walked, rode horses, or traveled in those little carts or farm wagons. I found just watching the daily activity exciting.

Sometimes I would run to the backyard between our living room and the warehouse, where we stored merchandise for the dry goods store and supplies for the pharmacy. There were trees in the yard, and once a year the lilac came into fragrant bloom. For weeks, the yard smelled heavenly. There were yellow, white, and red flowers that I could not identify. In the winter, when snow lay on the cobbled streets and the wind swept through, I was happiest in the back yard, protected from the wind and cold; or I might stay inside to avoid getting sick.

At night we lit the kerosene lamp and sat around the table talking over a supper of soup and bread. Sometimes we read or looked at family photographs. It was a cozy peaceful time. Although there might be squabbles among the younger children, it was a place of peace and love.

In the summer, during the hot, humid weather, we went to stay on a farm, living in a typical country house of baked adobe, with roofs of straw and stables behind the house. By contrast, our houses in town were made of brick, stone, or sometimes wood. Summers were a time of adventure when children could wander in the woods and fields and learn first hand about cows, sheep, dogs, cats, horses, and mules.

In the early 1930s, radio brought us news of the outside world. At home, my parents and the older children began talking more about that man Hitler and the persecution of Jews that was beginning in Germany. The Germans blamed economic problems on the Jews, who were not large enough in number to protest. Many Jews owned businesses that brought in a large annual income, and Hitler was jealous. He vowed to make Germany the greatest country in the world, but a country in which Jews would play no role. In April of 1933, the boycott of Jewish business establishments officially began. Germans were prohibited from patronizing Jewish doctors, dentists, and lawyers. By April 1935, Jewish children were expelled from all German schools. Later that year the Nuremberg Laws deprived Jews of almost all civil rights. Little by little the Nazis took everything the Jews had, and soon began to ship them out of the country to work camps. As a little boy I became interested in the news and watched my father read of events with a pained expression on his face. When he finished, it was my turn to read the newspaper. I was stunned and disbelieving. Thousands of Jews had lost their jobs and businesses and were leaving Germany for other countries.

My parents and friends discussed these events. How could this happen in Germany, where so many people were educated professionals—doctors, lawyers, and businessman? What, I asked, could we do if the Germans were to invade Poland?

Where could we escape to safety? My parents answer was that this would never happen. Poland was strong enough to resist aggressors; they advised me not to worry. Still, my brother Peretz did not agree with them. He foresaw that Poland would be attacked and suggested that the family move to Russia. My parents convinced him that Poland was our home and in Russia we would have nothing. Besides that, we knew Russia had a history of terrible pogroms against the Jews.

However, the situation in Poland grew worse. The Poles themselves hated the Jews. My brother went on a buying trip to Warsaw and was attacked on the train. The Polish government built a bridge in our city, but no Jews were allowed to use it. We were attacked by a mob of Poles. For months at a time we dared not open the store because, as Jews, we would be assaulted, although ninety-five percent of Nowy Korczyn was Jewish. They painted signs on our doors saying, DON'T BUY AT JEWISH STORES. Friday and Saturday were the worst days because the Poles ran through the streets breaking windows and doors. They also robbed and assaulted us. On Sunday, they drank and marched through the city singing: "Jews to Palestine, Jews the capitalists, send away the Jews, Poland doesn't need or want them."

Those were frightening years I will never forget. I was attending a Polish school. When we Jews would go out, other students attacked us with sticks, bars, and stones. Many days I did not even want to go to school because of those hoodlums. We would get beaten and sometimes badly injured.

That was the picture of Poland that replaced the peaceful scenes of my early childhood. For me the years 1937 through 1939 were filled with fear, anger, and uneasiness; a period no one can comprehend except those who experienced it. The entire world looked on and listened, and in the end, did nothing.

CHAPTER II

The Debacle Begins

November 9, 1938 was a major turning point in the Nazi quest to exterminate the Jews. This night was called *Kristallnacht* or the "Night of the Broken Glass." The German people, led by the Nazis, stormed through Jewish communities in cities and towns throughout Germany. They burned buildings, smashed windows, and destroyed Jewish houses of worship. The Germans demolished 191 synagogues and destroyed 171 dwellings and 815 stores. Thirty thousand Jewish men were arrested and sent off to concentration camps, never to see their families again. Countless women were raped and 104 Jews were killed.

At this time the Nazi government was making plans to temporarily hold the Jews until they could decide what to do with them. They schemed to keep them in a closed-off section of the city in which they lived, called a ghetto. In Poland, there were three million Jews, more than in any other country. Therefore, after the German invasion and conquest of Poland in 1939, the largest ghettoes were to be found there.

Anti-Semitism grew in Poland as it did in Germany. There was a woman by the name of Pristo, the minister of agriculture, who wanted to abolish the slaughtering of animals according to Jewish ritual. Jewish law required that a *shochet* or ritual slaughter killed the animals with the least possible suffering to them. A Jewish senator, Greenbaum, fought against Pristo's ruling, but Jews could only follow *Kashrut* in secret.

Before the war broke out, Beck, the minister of defense, who was of German descent, ordered the head of the air force to ground all Polish planes, supposedly to ready them for war with Germany. When the Germans attacked Poland, the first

THE BURNING OF
"KRISTHAL NACHT"

1938

thing they did was destroy these planes on the ground, ending the possibility of any counter attack from the air. Thus, the Germans were able to advance rapidly into Poland.

Early on the morning of September 1, 1939, when I was ten years old, we heard planes roaring over the city. Alarmed, my parents ran out of the house and returned with grim faces. What they had seen were German planes with the dreaded sign of the Swastika. The announcement soon blared over the radio. The German Army has attacked Poland. Neighbors gathered and we all talked, and then waited for the newspaper to confirm the invasion of Poland. Day in and day out we heard and saw the German planes flying at such speed that it scared us all.

We carried on business as best we could, but we knew the days were numbered before the Germans arrived. The papers headlined each city taken by the Germans, some without any resistance. The war was real and at our doorstep.

The Jewish people of the city became scared and they abandoned their homes to go to other cities with the hope that the Germans would not catch up with them. But after a few days they caught up with them, and though the Jews were frightened, they returned to their homes.

The Polish soldiers were also on the run. Within a week, they were five kilometers from Nowy Korczyn. The soldiers looked for one hiding place after another, confused because their leaders had vanished. There was turmoil in the Polish Army.

My cousin was in the army and his battalion came tramping through our town. He came to us the day before the German Army arrived. He was hungry and exhausted, and at first we did not recognize him. We asked him to stay with us, but he said he had to defend our country. My father looked at him in despair, "You cannot fight the German Army; it is too strong, and Poland is a sellout. In three to four weeks Poland will be overrun."

Peretz shook his head and said, "I have to try, we have to try."

We begged and pleaded with him, but he was firm. He stayed with us for supper that Friday night, enjoying our usual Sabbath meal of gefilte fish, chicken noodle soup, chicken, and dessert.

My cousin didn't want to stay because he was afraid of being accused of desertion from the army, so he said, "Goodbye, goodbye forever," while embracing us in farewell.

That was our last Friday night under the Polish government. All that night we sat in the cellar and waited. We heard the roaring noises of machinery but did not know where they were coming from. My father and mother gave us what comfort they could, not really knowing what to say. My father told us stories throughout the night. I still remember one story in particular, which occurred during the First World War.

My father was a boy of ten living in the same house as his grandparents. The Russians were fighting the Poles and the city was a battleground; hundreds of

MY COUSIN, (A POLISH SOLDIER) HIS LAST VISIT. SEPT. — 1939

our soldiers and townspeople were killed. There was hand-to-hand fighting with bayonets and thousands were wounded; the streets were bloody. Some Polish soldiers broke into the house and locked the door. The Russians came and split the door and struck a Pole in the chest, but the door did not yield. Finally the Russian soldiers went on their way. There was no way the family could save that wounded soldier. He told my grandparents his name and address; he happened to be Jewish. While the battle raged on, he murmured, "Hear, oh Israel, the Lord our G-d, the Lord is one," and then he died.

The leader of that battle was Jozef Pilsudski. The Russians tried to capture him but did not succeed. A Jewish family named Orbach hid him. They saved his life. It took several months after that before the war ended and Poland won independence.

Poland was restored as a country, with new borders established and a new government formed. The leader became Jozef Pilsudski, the very man who was saved by that Jewish family. Our city was declared to be a historical one and a special monument was erected by that house. The house was remodeled and made into a palace, and people came from all over to see where their leader had been saved and by whom. How? By an old Jewish remedy. The Orbach's had given him women's clothing to change his appearance; and though the Russians came to the house and turned it upside down in their hunt, they did not find him. Wearing his disguise, Pilsudski was sweeping the floor as they hunted! The Russians left in a rage, saying they would get him eventually and send him to Russia for trial. When they left the house, Pilsudski donned his uniform and became a general again, departing for an unknown destination.

"Don't forget this story," my father said. "It was Jews who helped to save him and our country."

Early the next morning the sounds of battle died away. My father went upstairs to look outside and saw the street was deserted, except for a few soldiers walking. They were the last of the retreating Polish Army. Soon after that, we heard motorcycles, shooting, explosions, and other noises coming nearer and nearer. It was the advance of the German Army. My father came down to the cellar to reassure us. "Don't be frightened. We'll be all right." Nevertheless, the younger children were sobbing out of fear.

We waited and waited as the army marched into our Nowy Korczyn. We could not believe it, but it was happening. Interpreters shouted out in Polish to the townspeople, "Come out, come out and go to the marketplace." We were all afraid but there was no choice. We went to the marketplace where we saw many of our friends and people of all ages gathered together. We stood there for hours; some were so exhausted they fell asleep on the floor of the market.

Suddenly, a jeep drove up with six military men and two civilians. We knew the civilians; they were Germans who had settled among us years earlier. One, by the name of Frederick, had worked for us in our pharmacy in 1938 and had built a home for himself and his family in our city. Until that day, we did not know he was a German spy. He spoke through a microphone to the Jews crowded together in the marketplace.

"Don't be afraid. As long as you do what you are told and cooperate with us, you will not be harmed. Do you understand?"

We answered yes, and said we would obey. What else could we do? We were afraid to say no. The large German Army marched through the city, all-powerful with tanks and armored cars; planes flew overhead. They had a good, disciplined standing army.

It was Saturday morning—the Sabbath day—a day of special observance and prayer; but this was a terrifying day for us and our fellow Jews. We made up most of the population of the city. While we stood there in the marketplace, we heard the steady drone of planes, the clanking of machinery, and the voices of the passing German soldiers. We didn't know what would happen next. I'll never forget that Saturday.

At noon on September 9, 1939, the commander arrived. He had an outline of procedures. The interpreter called our three names and announced that these three men would be responsible for everything the German Army asked for. Among the three, all of whom were well-to-do merchants, was my father. When they called his name, we all began to cry and my mother fainted. When she regained consciousness she cried because she feared she would never see him again. My brothers and sisters and I said goodbye to him. It was just like taking a piece of our world away from us all. Then the interpreter, standing in the marketplace surrounded by machine-gunners, read out the instructions:

"Anybody who has hidden any Polish soldiers, let us know. Anybody who has guns or rifles, bring them to us here. If any of you know someone who has hidden soldiers or has guns, let us know. We are holding these men hostage while you go home and bring us all the sugar, salt, gold, and diamonds you have. Until you have brought all these things to us we will keep these men hostage."

The city was in a panic; we didn't know what to do. Should we give a part of what we had or all of it? Most of us gave some and kept the rest for a future day. Even though we knew the lives of the hostages were in danger, we took the chance. Thank G-d, they accepted our word and believed us, and the hostages were freed. As that Sabbath drew to a close, we experienced true Sabbath joy as we prayed and thanked G-d for returning our father to us unharmed.

For almost a week businesses were closed until the situation normalized. Little by little shops opened and business went on as usual, but the underlying fear was tremendous. In time, the Germans established their government over us and issued new orders. Businessmen and peddlers were told not to go out of town on business without a permit. If they were caught, they would be shot. Some of our friends were caught and shot on the spot.

Life continued with fear. A permit was needed for any travel and a special permit was required to buy merchandise. Some of these were not honored and those people never returned. Luckily my oldest brother, Harry, went on buying trips many times and G-d protected him. He traveled to Tarnow, Kraknow, Lodz, and Warsaw, and several times was attacked by Poles on the train. Even though he was traveling with a permit, they took away his personal belongings. Finally, my brother decided he should not travel anymore. He managed to survive the war and later lived with his family in Chicago.

Most of us, including my father, worked at hard labor during the German occupation. We worked on highways, built bridges and camps, and cleaned the streets. We had no contact with the outside world; communication was completely cut off. A smuggled-in newspaper was our only link to the outside world. Some courageous people left town in the middle of the night to seek shelter elsewhere. We never knew what tomorrow would bring. Every morning we went to work, not knowing whether we would return. Some of our young boys ran as far as the border between Russian-occupied and German-occupied Poland. The biggest river, the Bug, partially formed this border. Some boys made it across and others disappeared without a trace. I was always on the alert. There wasn't much I could do, but I always used common sense. I was polite and tried to please the Germans, working any place they wanted me. In order to stay alive in those years, 1939 and 1940, I did everything according to instructions.

CHAPTER III

The Yellow Stars

In the year 1941, every Jewish person in Nazi-occupied Poland had to wear an armband with a Jewish star, the Star of David. For us it was dangerous. Most of us were afraid to put it on; we were afraid to walk out with the star because to be recognized endangered our lives. My brother Peretz was a fighter and he refused to wear the armband. He sold merchandise through our store's back doors and traveled illegally as a gentile. I took chances running from place to place down the side streets to get food and other necessities for the family. Some youngsters were caught and sent away, never to be heard from or seen again. These were my friends, schoolmates with whom I grew up and played. Some of our friends were shot on the spot when caught.

Those days of fear are engraved in my heart, and I can never forget what happened to my friends, my family, and my home. At this time my brother Peretz wanted to start an underground group to combat what was going on. This group was to consist of his friends and others who wanted to retaliate. His plan was not successful because the people were afraid and they didn't have any weapons. The Poles would not help in any way. Communications were completely severed, even from the Polish underground.

The Poles formed ghettos throughout the cities of Poland. I never knew what a ghetto was, but I soon found out. A ghetto consisted of a few city blocks surrounded by walls and German guards. Conditions in the ghettos were horrible, and diseases spread rapidly. Sanitation was lacking because sewer systems did not function and there were no outhouses. Living quarters were so cramped that each family was limited to one room, maybe two for a large family. The Nazis

Replica of a Jewish armband.

rationed out food, but it was not enough. Water was available, but it was usually contaminated.

Jews were not permitted to practice their religion openly, so they were forced to practice it in secret. The German police began arresting Jews for the smallest offense. Of those arrested, the strong were sent to labor camps and the weak were usually taken outside the ghetto walls and shot. The Nazis deceived the Jews by instructing the Jewish leaders in the ghettos to list families they could call on when new jobs opened up in the city. These people were sent off to concentration and labor camps instead of to the city and jobs. These Jews were the first inmates of extermination camps.

No one could enter or leave the ghetto. No one could bring anything in except through the gates, which the Germans guarded. Some few escaped to other cities. Some were gunned down like sheep. We kept expecting something to happen to us, but we didn't know what or when.

In 1940 my father built a bunker in our warehouse. No one knew except the family, and he warned us that no one must know; he was a learned man who looked to the future. "Someday we will use it," he told us.

In the warehouse in the back of our house, we built a double wall so that if the Germans' broke the first wall, they would not get to us. There was a secret entrance from the attic; it was covered with straw and dirt to conceal it. "I hope we never have to use it," my father said. As it turned out, we did, to try to save our lives.

Secretly we held religious services in our basement or that of our neighbors. Friday night we always had the candle-lighting ceremony and a special meal for family and friends. My mother was very careful to observe religious rituals; she saw that everything was done properly. We were a large family with relatives from other parts of Poland, and they stayed with us. The Poles didn't like it, so for various reasons they informed on us. They hated us even more than the Germans themselves. We were always the most alert on Friday nights.

One Friday the Polish police, along with the German SS, marched on the street where we lived. They stopped in front of the store and knocked on the door. When we did not answer, they knocked louder and louder. Finally they knocked on the door of our house, which had a separate entrance through a hallway at the side of the store. They knocked so loud that we decided to open it; it was my sister Luba who opened the door. They stormed in like enraged beasts. They saw the lighted Sabbath candles in a gleaming silver candelabrum, a white tablecloth, a challah with a cover over it, the fine china dishes, and a table set with sterling silver. In the traditional manner, everyone was dressed in his or her Sabbath best, preparing to give thanks to G-d and welcome the Sabbath.

My father was dressed in a black suite with a white shirt and tie, and his long light-brown beard was the adornment he loved more than any jewelry. My mother wore a beautiful lace dress and *sheitel*, or wig, on her head and looked like a queen. Everybody was sitting at his or her place with pride. Besides our family of nine children and parents, my uncle and aunt were there with their two children.

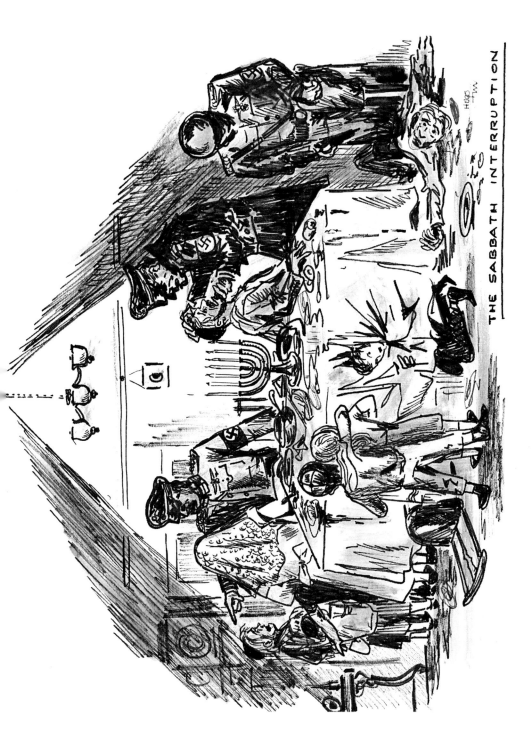

15

The Polish police and the SS men walked over to my father and grabbed him by his beard, pulling him away from the table. Enraged my brother, Peretz, screamed at the Germans and held onto my father. One German pulled out a gun and holding it to his head shouted, "One more move and you will be dead." Another intervened and ordered by brother to lie on the floor face down as he held a gun to Peretz's head. My mother fell at the German's knees and begged him not to harm him. She cried bitterly and prayed for mercy on his soul. All of us were afraid.

Later they told my father this time they would forgive him for observing Sabbath rituals. They commanded my mother to tell her son not to be so stupid and ignorant. My father was white, scared, and in shock when the Germans brought him back after questioning him outside. He couldn't talk or tell us what had taken place, and he was shaking. We all cried, though we didn't know what happened. Finally, he began to speak in a shaky voice and told us they wanted him to go down to German headquarters on Monday morning. He wept for two days from fright.

On Monday morning he prayed to G-d to spare his life. He kissed the Mezuzah* and said, "May G-d watch over my going out and my coming in from now and evermore." He said goodbye to us with hopes that we would see him again. Our prayer to G-d was that we should see him alive again in our home. With that he left the house. Two hours later we saw him plodding weakly down the street. We hardly recognized him! They had shaved off his beard! They had beaten him so badly he could barely walk. We ran out to help him home and laid him in his bed. He was weeping and said that he didn't want to live. We talked to him, others talked to him, and finally we persuaded him that this was not the worst thing that could have happened. Since he still had his life, in time everything would heal and he would be all right. It was more than five weeks before the wounds and scars had faded away. Finally he became normal and life went on.

---

* A small roll of parchment on which is written the Shema and two biblical passages concerning the love for G-d and His precepts. Enclosed in a metal or wooden case, the Mezuzah is fastened in a slanting position to the upper part of the door-post on the right side of the entrance.

CHAPTER IV

The Bunker

Sunday, November 22, 1942, the whole city was surrounded by SS, Polish police, and soldiers from the Ukraine and elsewhere—all helping the Nazis to annihilate the Jewish people. That was another I will never forget. People were sobbing and wailing, knowing in their hearts and souls that this was the end of their homes and families. Even the children and grandchildren began weeping. We all knew our dreams had ended, our future vanished, and these were our last moments with friends, family, and neighbors. But those friends, neighbors, and relatives still live in my mind and my heart. All night long we said our farewells to each other. It was a world we would never see again—a world of love, of trust, of neighborliness, kindness, and peace.

My brother Moses had a girlfriend. When my father signaled that it was time for us to retreat to the bunker which he carefully had prepared for such an emergency, my brother came to us and said quietly that he was going with her wherever she might go and share her fate, whatever it might be. We said a final farewell to him.

Even safely hidden in our bunker we were afraid; we heard screaming, crying, shouting, and shooting. Yet, we had taken this step for better or for worse, hoping that we could remain together as a family. We could hear men as they searched our house because our family had not shown up for the march with the rest of the town's Jews. Then we heard them in the garden and the warehouse, and we heard them yell that if they found us they would punish us with death. We all knew what our destiny would be if we were caught, but together we prayed to G-d to save us. We could not talk; we whispered. We were paralyzed with fear; we sat like statues, hardly moving, looking at each other as if these were our last moments of life. We heard a voice say, "We found them." We heard soldiers breaking down the first wall, but they searched no further. A Polish officer said, "They must have left the city before we surrounded it."

We heard them tramping out and my father wondered if it was a trick. For a full day we didn't move. Suddenly we heard the meowing of a cat. We found out later that a guard had been left behind in case we showed up. That night it began to rain. While the wind howled and the rain poured down, with thunder and lightning, we could talk and move around a little. On the fourth day my father said we could not remain confined in the bunker indefinitely. We had to find some solution to our problem.

He looked at us children and said gravely, "One of us must volunteer to leave the premises in order to find some solution. But, if you are caught, you must not disclose where you came from, even to save your life." It was my brother Peretz who volunteered. "I'll go with G-d's guidance, in good faith." On our sixth day in the bunker he left at 4:00 A.M., after we had all hugged him and bid him goodbye, and my father had blessed him.

Another week passed. We were running out of food and we could not move around. We were getting desperate, wondering how long we could last like this. If nothing happened to save us, we would finally have to give ourselves up, leaving our destiny in G-d's hands. On the ninth day we debated what to do next. My father sighed and said the time had come to send out another person. This time one of my sisters, Chana, volunteered. At dawn the next morning my father blessed her and embraced her, and we said our goodbyes. She left with the hope that through the grace of G-d that she would find her brother and together they would work out a solution.

It was hot in the bunker. We were out of food; there was no toilet or shower, and the odor was overpowering. In our desperation my father continually repeated that G-d was with us; He would not forsake us; He would send us salvation. We would not surrender to the Germans, for they would kill us like animals. He persuaded us to wait one more day—our fifteenth day in the bunker. On that rainy day we fetched some water to sustain us. As we closed the entrance, we heard footsteps approaching. Desperate as we were, and so frightened, this time we hardly cared. The footsteps stopped and then we heard three knocks, a prearranged signal, and the voice of our brother called out: "It's Peretz. I am back. Open up, Father."

Needless to say we felt great relief and joy as we opened the door to let him in. Then he told us his story. He had passed through the city uninterrupted, and headed for the main highway. In the distance he heard a horse and buggy. He was scared but determined to stop the traveler. It was someone who recognized him and called him by name. The man then asked how he had gotten there. Peretz replied that he had been left on the highway and was walking home. The man told him that the Germans had left a few people in the city. They were tailors, shoemakers, bakers, locksmiths, doctors, and the head of the ghetto, Raca, with his family. He

18

explained that the Germans had formed a small ghetto for those people.

When they rode toward the city the man, Joshek, told Peretz to hide under the seat. He was breaking the law by hiding him. German soldiers were passing by, but not realizing that his life was at risk, he took a chance and did something most Poles would have feared to do. Joshek was truly a man of courage. There were many people in the market-square as we entered. "Peretz, this is the time to get off," he said. "Go straight to Leib Raca, the leader in the ghetto."

Peretz at once headed toward Raca's house; then in the distance he saw German soldiers. He was frightened but he continued walking past them. After what seemed an eternity, he reached the house and knocked on the door. When it finally opened, the president recognized him. He was shocked and fearful. Peretz stood in front of partly opened door while being questioned. "How did you get here? Did anyone see you?"

"No, no one," Peretz assured Raca, and they went inside. President Raca was astonished and asked if he were alone.

"Yes," Peretz replied. "I'm alone but my family is still hidden in the bunker and we need help. Can you help us, Mr. Raca?"

Raca paced back and forth in the living room, thinking. "I'm in a terrible position, Peretz. I don't see how we can do anything but bring you to the police and the Gestapo and say you were left on the highway and the only place you knew to go was Nowy Korczyn ghetto."

It was a big risk, but Peretz agreed to do whatever the president thought best. Two days later he left in the middle of the night with two Jewish police officers from the ghetto. They walked behind stone walls, hoping the Germans would not see them. Moving cautiously toward our old home in the dark of the night, they reached the main street entrance, glanced around, and listened for footsteps echoing in the streets. Finally my brother jumped the fence, climbed up the stone building, and called out quietly to the family. "It's Peretz, father! I've come to take you out of the bunker."

My father opened the door with joy upon hearing Peretz's voice. But, after embraces and some weeping, he cried. "My son, my son, where can we go?" My mother and sisters wept as they too embraced Peretz. Peretz tried to reassure them. I was so happy to see him again, but at the same time all of us were frightened, both of leaving or remaining in that bunker.

"Father, father, don't worry," Peretz urged. "We'll all be together. Come, we must go because the police are waiting and we have little time."

"Police! Are you out of your mind, Peretz?" My father demanded, more frightened than ever.

My brother put an arm around him and said again, "Don't worry, everything is arranged and so far we are safe."

What else could we do but trust Peretz and the president? We were at our wit's end. We walked carefully, taking every precaution, staying close together, most of us arm in arm. We heard dogs barking and cats meowing, and we were scared every step of the way. In the distance we heard footsteps that sounded like the Gestapo marching in the streets.

By sundown we arrived at the ghetto. The next morning my father went to talk with the president to discuss our situation. The president could only say, "You must report to the Gestapo office as we agreed. We'll tell them the story of how you were left on the highway and didn't know where else to go."

So the following morning, in trepidation, we all reported to the Gestapo office, accompanied by the president. "Where were you when we were looking for you?" The Gestapo office demanded, as we shook in our boots. "We marched all the Jews out of the city."

"We were the first ones on the march," my father answered in a quivering voice. None of us knew what might happen next. We feared our lives were nearing an end and our minutes numbered. Then the leader of the SS arrived, and our hearts sank. I searched my mind for some course of action I might take; but with my family present, I could not act alone. By now we were all visibly shaking.

In dread we looked at the photograph in the office. Larger than life, it was of that man whose name we had first heard scarcely more than a dozen years before—Hitler! We recalled our belief that whatever happened in Germany could not possibly happen in Poland. Two hours later an SS officer strode in, elegant in his shining boots and polished insignia, yet arrogant and terrifying. We stood trembling in front of him, while he read the verdict in a bored monotone. "You are permitted to stay in the ghetto only for the purpose of working until further notice from the German government."

Reprieved, we fell at his feet in joy to thank him for saving our lives, at least for the present.

CHAPTER V

The Ghetto

In the ghetto we had to obey all the rules and regulations of the German government, but we knew we would not survive there for long. Fearful of what each new day might bring, we made plans to escape, hoping to join the underground resistance. Finally, after two and half months, we devised a plan of action, including a time limit for carrying it out.

One week before that time limit was to expire, an order came from the head of the Polish Army to liquidate the ghetto. We were to be transported to a ghetto in Sandomiez. Jews were to be gathered there from smaller ghettos all over southern Poland. This time we knew it would be our last journey; it would be the end of us. My brother Peretz, then nineteen; my sister Chana, fifteen; and I thirteen, though still teenagers, were determined we would escape to fight for survival. We begged our younger brother Israel to come with us, but he refused. I will never forget his words: "Wherever my parents go, I will go with them."

On that Sunday, October 20, 1942, all of us sobbing and weeping, held on to each other, knowing we would never see each other again. Like Abraham blessing his sons, my father blessed us. "Let G-d be with you and show you the way of survival from the Nazis, and when you do survive, don't forget who your parents were."

With tears streaking down our cheeks, looking longingly at our parents and siblings, we kissed them and finally tore ourselves away. We knew we would be fighting for our lives in order to preserve our destiny as Jews against the Germans. We now knew that millions of innocent Jews had died at their hands.

We crept out through the rear of the ghetto along a passageway we had found.

First we went to the house of a former customer, Paul. Despite the danger to himself and his family, he took us up to his attic and let us stay there. There were bundles of straw in the attic. In the distance we could see our beloved family and friends as they began a march to an unknown destination, trudging together in bitter cold through the deep snow. We were cold in the attic, but we huddled together, sharing a couple of blankets and trying to keep warm with hot coffee and hot soup. We knew the Germans were looking for Jews who had escaped. They were very methodical about keeping track of us, and they were looking for whatever wealth was left behind. We paid Paul's family well, but that would be no compensation if they were found out.

It was a frustrating, miserable week. We left Nowy Korczyn in early November after arranging with some Polish police to transfer us to our destination. We had to cross both the Nida River and the Vistula, and since it was too cold to swim, we had to go by boat. From the bunker to the river we tramped a mile and a half through the snow, looking fearfully around every corner and constantly checking behind us, not knowing when some Nazi might descend on us.

The bridge was secured by the German SS. Even though all four of the Polish police were armed and prepared for the worst, we had to find a way to elude the Germans. Slowly and quietly we moved toward the boat. Suddenly a blizzard came upon us, hiding us from the SS just as we were getting into the boat and slipping across the river. On the opposite shore we lay down on the snow, exhausted by our efforts, and rested, spreading out to be less noticeable.

Ten minutes later we began the second half of the journey. As we neared the Vistula after a three-mile walk, we saw more German patrols. Though the security was tight, we knew we had to continue on and that our Polish guards would continue to help us.

They knew the exact time for the changing of the guards. At that precise moment we jumped into our boats and were able to cross the Vistula in a matter of minutes, knowing our very lives were at stake. Although we were forty-five minutes late, we found those who were to meet us still waiting. We paid off our escorts and stepped out of the boat into a horse-drawn buggy.

We drove through forests, along small rivers, and through tiny villages until we reached our destination an hour later. A mile further on we got off in the middle of the forest and traveled on foot so no one would hear us. No one heard anything, not even the animals. When we came to the house, at last, the owner had a dog, but he was trained to follow commands. Since this house was in the middle of the village, we approached it from the rear through the fields and walked slowly into the owner's barn. He was there waiting for us. His name was Janek Dombrowsky. He was married with four children, the oldest a daughter of fourteen and the youngest a boy of four. His family never knew we were there; we stayed in the barn until spring, in a tiny room he had made measuring about three by four by six feet.

There was little to do but lie there. The floor was covered with straw to deaden noise, and the doorway was covered with a bundle of straw. Only the owner knew where it was. We could not walk out. He brought us food in the dark of night so nobody could see him taking anything inside. We ate in the dark, whispered to each other in the dark, and did everything in the dark. We became so used to it that we forgot what lights were like.

It was winter and snow fell much of the time. We were cold inside, cold all over, and the two blankets we had weren't enough to keep us warm. Each morning we did some exercises inside the barn, then washed up with snow or ice water. It was a terrible life, full of boredom and always marked by fear. We never knew when a fatal knock might come.

Each morning the owner came to brief us on the news or bring us a Polish paper to read. He was a Communist who hated the takeover of Poland. Sometimes he worked with the underground and he was able to tell us about developments in Russia; he managed to keep our hopes high despite everything.

We were cloistered in that tiny room until the spring of 1943. Then Dombrowsky built a bunker inside his house where we would be better protected. It was located in his workshop and wooden flooring covered it; the entrance was through a clothes closet. It was beautiful, but we could not stand up or walk around, so most of the time we lay down. He gave us all kinds of books and papers to read, and since we had prayer books, my brother taught me how to read and translate Hebrew. We were even given a kerosene lamp for light when we needed it. At night we emerged from the bunker into the shop and walked around to stretch our legs.

In spite of all the books, it was a nerve-racking experience. Being pent up together does not promote social graces; we all grew testy and short-tempered, though we tried hard to control ourselves. Fear is a hard master. We were fatigued from the strains and claustrophobia, grateful though we were to have a space of any kind in which to exist. Hope is what kept us sane.

Maybe tomorrow we would be free, like other people. Whenever the owner brought us a paper from the Polish underground, we would read about how many resistance fighters had died. We thanked G-d that we were still alive, though He alone knew for how long.

A great event occurred in 1943 while we were in that bunker. We received some mail from a friend of our parents. He lived about six miles from our hiding place but didn't know where we were. Once a month after that we waited to get our mail and eagerly sent letters to that friend. He wrote us that they had enough food, a place to sleep, and friends around them. They said the German government was going to send them to Palestine, our homeland.

We looked at each other. Was this really possible? Maybe we would join that friend. It sounded so much better than our tiny little bunker. Peretz shook his head and said violently, "No, it's a trap. Don't you see? It's propaganda to lure us out of hiding. Then we'd be sent to the gas chambers. Would you take that risk?" We looked at him sheepishly and said no, but we longed to believe that fairy tale.

Every so often we would send a messenger to the ghetto to find out how our parents were, and we received letters and regards from them. One day I told Chana and Peretz that I wanted to go with the messenger to see for myself how the family was. I could then give them news of us firsthand. I started out on the journey disguised as a Christian boy, the son of the messenger. We traveled three days by horse and buggy to Sandomiez, one of the largest ghettos in Poland. Finally, I was smuggled into the ghetto to see my parents.

The situation was terrible. They worked every day and slept on the floor. No one knew when they would be leaving. They clung desperately to rumors that they would be sent to Palestine. I warned my parents what Peretz had said, that is was a trick to lure all the Jews back into the ghetto, and then they would send everyone to another unknown destination.

"Where can we go?" cried my father.

"What will happen to us here?" my mother asked, weeping.

"G-d's will," I said, trying to comfort them. "If we try to help ourselves, G-d will help us survive the struggle and once again we will be together, free."

I stayed with them for a month and on the last day felt dreadfully depressed. Many family friends were there too, but no one knew what would happen next. People were heartbroken as they mourned parents, children, other family members, and friends who had already been taken from the ghetto.

I asked them, "Do you know where they have gone? They were sent to some unknown place. May G-d be with them." We were afraid to talk about what we thought had really happened to them.

I pleaded with my younger brother and sister to come with me, but they would not leave our parents. I hated to leave, too, and stayed on longer than I had planned. We ate what we could—soup each day with two slices of bread; it was much more than I expected. We were allowed buy extra food on the black market if we had the money.

In August, the Germans announced there would be an exodus out of the ghetto. They told us not to take many belongings because the trip would be short and we would not need much. I decided to stick with my family no matter what. We began our march to the train station, which took nearly two hours. People fell, unable to walk, and were taken away. My mother and father struggled vainly to walk until finally we had to take them under our arms and drag them to the station. There was no pity for us, whether we were young or old. The Polish police were mean, the Ukrainians were worse, and the Germans pushed and beat us. They knew our destination.

In spite of the mistreatment and suffering, hope did not die within us. Seeing a train in the distance, we said eagerly, "Look, look, this must be the train that will take us to Palestine! We'll go to the future homeland for the Jews and we'll be free!"

With all our strength we rushed to line up to be first on the train; then I saw the Germans with machine guns, rifles, and pistols. With cruelty they packed us into those box cars like cattle. We could hardly move. They had placed chemicals inside and locked the doors on us. There was hardly any air. There were even military personnel with machine guns even on top of the train.

Now we were worse off than ever. We couldn't get enough air to breathe. People began to faint. We tried with all our might to break a window and were finally able to force one open. When I saw my parents faint, I realized there was no choice but to jump for it, though I heard machine guns. I didn't care; I was desperate. One man jumped before me; then I jumped and shots were fired at me. I fell flat on the ground, hoping they would believe I was dead. I felt blood running down my leg against my woolen pants, but realized I could not move until the train passed by and darkness fell.

I lay motionless throughout that wretched afternoon. Finally, I spotted a man walking in the field and ran to catch up with him. He, too, had jumped the train. We walked together for two days. His name was David Borshey. He told me he had friends who were in hiding and that he knew where to find them. He gave me directions on how to reach the town where I was born. From there I knew how to find the bunker in which I had been hiding with my brother, sister, and friend. I was so lucky that they were all in the same place.

Each night I trudged through the fields. I ate what I could find on the ground. In the daytime I lay under tress, in the fields, or in barns, resting and hiding. Often dogs barked and people looked to see who was around. G-d showed me the way to survive and the route to my destination.

Finally, I reached the city in the middle of the night. I went to a man I knew, but he did not recognize me until I told him my name. At last, he let me into his house. Before I jumped the train my father had given me some money with his blessings and said, "Go my child, and save yourself. I don't need any money. Take it all."

So I explained why I was there and told the man I could pay him to help me get across the two rivers again. I had enough money and arrangements were made. I chose Tuesday for the day of departure because my parents had always said that Tuesday was a lucky day. We left at two in the morning and they delivered me safely across both rivers. Then I paid him. I was afraid but there was no choice; it was either this or give myself up to the SS. I would rather die in battle than surrender to the Nazis.

All day I lay hidden under bushes. When it was completely dark and there were no lights in the homes, I traveled. I heard dogs barking, cats meowing, and sometimes I had to lie down and remain still because dogs ran around the fields. When I didn't move, they did me no harm and they stopped barking.

I crawled on my knees for miles. There was little left of the night, but from a distance I recognized the house. The owner's dog came racing up and I gave him something to eat. Recognizing me, he stopped barking when I called him by name. I continued crawling until I reached the house.

The owner had guessed who it was from the dog's reaction. When I finally opened the gate and walked in, he was waiting for me and asked how I got there.

THE ESCAPE

He took me inside and then broke the news that my brother, sister, and friend had to leave because the village was gossiping about his hiding Jews. But, he said, my brother should be back this week.

Most of the time I hid in the fields, but the owner knew where I was. Saturday night my brother and sister returned. Peretz knew that I had gone to some unknown destination and feared that I would never come back. Thus, seeing me again in that field was the surprise of his life.

While I was gone, Peretz had contacted more friends in the underground. The days and months dragged on. We got very tired and bored, but we still cherished hope. Some friends were only ten or fifteen miles away. Once a month one of us would meet them, and at other times they sent someone to meet with us to discuss the situation. We were determined to continue the struggle until we were liberated from our oppressors.

On May 15, 1943, the owner came running with shocking news. "Your friends were shot to death and found floating in the river downstream—the whole family, with seven children and two of their friends."

That day we could not eat, being so overcome with grief. We never knew who killed them. Some said it was the Polish underground fighters, others said it was the Germans.

Three days later, in the middle of the night, we heard knocking on the window of the owner's house. Someone whispered, "It's me, I'm wounded, let me in." The owner recognized him and let him in after making sure no one was watching.

"Aren't you Stamerk?"

"Yes!"

"They told me you were dead."

"I'm wounded, not dead."

My brother came up from the bunker and exclaimed, "Thank G-d you're alive! We were told you were all dead."

"They were all killed but I was only wounded," said Stamrek.

CHAPTER VI

Stamrek's Story

"We had lived in that bunker for over two years," Stamrek told us. "It was the Polish underground that found us." He went on with his story:

"Come out one by one and no one will hurt unless you fight us," the commander ordered.

Since there were children among them, Stamrek, the leader, decided to come out with his hands up. The rest followed. After all had emerged, they were commanded to march toward the river. Once at the river, Stamrek foresaw what would happen and begged them to spare their lives, at least those of the children.

This was the Polish underground, known as the A.K. Army Krajorer. "We'll kill all the Jews," the commander said. "No one will survive." First they shot the children, then the parents, casting them all into the river. Stamrek was only wounded, and since he was a strong swimmer, he survived. He swam to each body, one by one, hoping to find someone alive, but they were all dead. Grief-stricken, he swam ashore.

Stamrek had been a captain in the Polish Army and understood the predicament he was in. It was nearly dawn, so he looked for a place to hide. In the distance, through the glimmering of dawn, he saw a barn; and though he could hardly walk, he finally reached it. He hid under the straw and stayed there all day. His clothes were soaked, he was wounded, and he wished desperately that he could be back with his family.

When the sun was high, he walked into the house and found no one at home. He changed into other clothes, took some food and drink for himself, and went back to his hiding place.

FROM DARKNESS TO SUNSHINE

On the second night he walked to the river, but there were no boats, and Nazis guarded the bridge. He decided to risk revealing himself to the owner of one of the boats, who recognized him and exclaimed, "We thought you were dead!"

"They were all killed, but I was only wounded and was able to swim to shore," Stamrek said. "Would you take me across the river? I beg you. I know how dangerous it is for you, but if you are willing, I'll give you my house in the city if I survive."

The boat owner took him across in broad daylight at the same time other Poles were making the crossing. Stamrek made believe he was in good health and spirits, laughing and joking so the guards would not recognize him.

Once across the river, he vanished into the forest and hid there all day. At midnight he began walking toward our house, taking care to make sure no one had followed him, and he crawled over to knock on the window. The frightened owner ran for his rifle and was ready to shoot. When he saw Stamrek about to fall to the ground, he decided it must be someone he knew. Running out the door, he found Stamrek lying on the ground bleeding.

Cautiously, he lifted Stamrek, dragged him inside, and laid him down on the floor. He used what medication and bandages he had and then notified us in the field.

My brother and sister ran to the house. They recognized him and said, "Thank G-d you're alive! Come, we'll help you and care for you." We were happy to add another to our team of freedom fighters, and we stayed together.

1943 was a year of horror, agony, and triumph. We knew the bunker we were in was no longer safe, so we discussed the possibility of building another one in the stable. We promised the owner more gold and money as long as we could stay with him. We would have to rely on him to provide potatoes, cabbages, fruits, and coal for the winter. The door to the stable would be left wide open so no one would be suspicious. The owner and his wife were alarmed more for their children than for themselves. We understood; it was months before the new bunker was finished and we moved in.

In the big barn there was a place for cattle and a separate section for the pigs. Besides eight or ten cows and ten to fourteen pigs, there were twenty rabbits and many other animals. We built the bunker so that it was impossible to see unless someone knew about it, but I was so small that all five of us could occupy it at the same time only in an emergency. It was only two by six feet. Dirty from pig manure, it always stunk; and the noise made by the pigs, snuffling and fighting while they ate drove us crazy. But our hopes for survival were high, so we put up with anything and everything. Through the outside we opened a board by using an inside hinge that swayed back and forth. The old barn could not be recognized because of its beaten-up condition and the work being done on it.

Inside the bunker, we made five seats without the benefit of nails, using little boards and straw. We could move only our heads and had to whisper or use gestures and sign language to communicate. All our belongings were stuffed under those little seats. We didn't have much because we didn't need much for that kind of life; we lived from day to day. Occasionally we were invited into the house for tea or coffee late at night while the kids slept and no one was on the street. We used little light so as not to arouse suspicion among the neighbors.

In those days we remembered something our parents had told us years earlier about a magic table. It could predict the future, or give you the answer to anything you wished to know. The owner had a table with wooden nails that served the function of that magic table. We sat four people on one side of the table and put our wrists on that side. After waiting a few minutes, we would say the magic words: *"Sehn guerther hern sugen se mir our zukunft"*—"Tell us the fate of our future, dear, oh fortune teller." It responded to our question and told us the truth by moving up and down on two legs.

If we asked how many years we would be in the bunker, it responded by lifting the table to one side, one per year. If we asked how old a person was, it went up on two legs that many times. When we asked how many would survive, it told us three people, but which three? Were we the only members living now? We were puzzled by the table's answer. We knew that my brother and my sister were in labor camps, but were they alive?

We looked at each other and said, "It must be wrong." We asked again and got the same reply. We couldn't understand. As time went by, we used the magic table repeatedly.

The table was right; only three of us made it, my brother Harry, my sister Sarah, and myself.

We heard about personal, national, and world problems during this time—and about the ghettos and concentration camps. We didn't know what each new day might bring.

WILL THEY EVER FIND US AMONGST THE PIG'S NOICE?

CHAPTER VII

More Risks

In December of 1943, before Christmas, the Nazis began another search for members of the Jewish underground. They examined a ten-mile area of forests, churches, houses, and other buildings. They searched every house on the block in that village, including ours.

They went into the house, and found the bunker we had first used. They stood around and looked, and one said, "Some suspicious place."

The owner was scared and tried to mask his feelings. Then they went into the barn. We sat like statues, scarcely breathing. We were worried because our friend had asthma, breathed with a rasp, and coughed a lot. We hoped he could control himself.

Peeping through the board we saw three men outside with machine guns, and there were others with them. They checked out the area with the cows, and then opened the door to the pigs, which were grunting and shuffling around in the dirt. The searchers shined their flashlights. "What a stink from those pigs," one of them said, "filthy place."

Another laughed. "Even the dirty Jews wouldn't hide here," he said.

As the SS men started to close the door and leave, our friend uttered a deep cough.

We thought it was all over. Then the pigs began to cough and the SS men laughed. "The pigs cough like Jews," one said, and as they went into the stable we heard them say again in German, "They really do cough like Jews!" At last they left.

It was a miracle from G-d. We were white, almost blue, from not breathing

SILENT AND SCARED.

during that time. We sat tight for another four or five hours while the search continued for the rest of the day.

At night the owner came to us and said, "I don't think they will come back here anymore."

However, the following day the Germans returned and searched the barn and the fields again. It was three days before they completed their search of the village.

The owner's wife became very frightened and said we would have to look for another place. It was a very difficult time because now the Russians as well as Germans were advancing into Poland.

We had other friends who were hiding in a bunker in a barn under the straw. The custom in Europe was to keep the barn filled with straw for the cows. There were five people in a five-foot-high bunker that was five feet deep and five feet long.

The Germans searched with bayonets, stabbing to check the height and depth all over. Our friends saw the edges of the bayonets plunging through the straw where they were lying on their backs praying to G-d. When it was over, they too thanked G-d for a miracle.

There was no room to join our friends, so we journeyed west. Luckily, we found another hiding place. It was the home of a young man and his twelve-year-old brother. We promised to pay him so much money a month, and he agreed. We made a little shelter out of straw with a double wall at the end of the attic. Unless one knew it were there, it was not recognizable.

Often we saw the Germans marching by on the highway and many times they searched the house for food, hoping to find Polish salami, considered the best in Europe. For several months we saw the German Army on maneuvers and watched them training men to operate the tanks. The training went on day after day while we sat in the bunker most of the time watching.

In late 1944, the German Army marched eastward toward the Russian front. The young man, Stack Ringel, after saving up the money we had paid him , began buying cows, pigs, new furniture, and other things. Neighbors began to talk and accused him of hiding Jews. The rumors spread through the village and he got scared. The Russians were advancing into Poland; and by the end of August 1944, we saw Russian patrols in the city. They came by boat down the river, and we saw them patrolling the grounds around the village. They went back and forth, so we could never be sure where they were.

Confused, we were afraid to go out. For several days it was like No Man's Land. Peretz said, "We've waited so long; we can wait a few more days until the situation clears up." Meanwhile, he wrote a speech that he wanted to deliver after our liberation, when we Jews would be free from oppression. He wrote it in Polish, Hebrew, and Yiddish. These were words written with blood and tears. The speech recounted what had happened to us: from life at home before the invasion to the months spent in the ghetto; the departure from the ghetto; life in the underground, where some of us made new friends; and finally the time spent in hiding, always wondering which of us would survive and find freedom. In his Freedom Speech, my brother said:

> Today is the day of liberation from the oppressors, the German Reich and the Polish underground, the so-called Freedom Fighters against the Jewish people, and the Germans.
>
> Today is the day we will remember as long as we shall live. Today is the day we will thank G-d for the freedom he has provided us.
>
> Today is the day we will memorialize the Jewish fighters who fought for their lives and fell in battle.
>
> Today is the day we will be able to tell the world what a struggle we had to go through for survival.

We listened to his words with tears rolling down our cheeks and we all embraced each other, hoping for that moment when we would finally be free again. These were days of real hope for the future, and we dreamed of a better time to come. But our hopes were crushed. The Russians pulled out and the Germans came back. The front lines were only a few miles from us, and we were at a stage when we had no idea what would happen next. We were afraid to ask the owner if he had heard anything new or had any idea what was going on. Now we were sorry we hadn't ventured out when the Russians came. We were at a critical point in our lives, which would shape our destiny.

Meanwhile the pounding of artillery and the rattling of machine guns grew louder as the battle approached. Tanks came thudding by every day. It was the rainy season and the rain poured down. The Germans set an 8:00 P.M. curfew; after that, any person out on the street had to suffer the consequences. It was dangerous for everyone, regardless of nationality. The highways and streets were filled with German troops and the military occupied every post.

Tears welled up in our eyes on those dark, rainy days. We were depressed and miserable. Our morale was the lowest ever. That week the owner came to us and said, "This is the last week that I can help you. I'm sorry, but it is too dangerous and the neighbors are accusing me of hiding Jews. It's dangerous for you too. You'll have to find another place."

We understood.

One member of our group had been born in that neighborhood, knew all the storekeepers there, and still had many friends. However, not one of them would take us in, even though we begged them and offered to pay anything for their help.

This man from our group returned Thursday night and told us he'd found a place where we could hide. He had been a friend with the owner since childhood. It was dangerous to move that Friday night, but we had no choice. We started walking at 4:00 A.M., found the friend, paid in advance for the month, and again went into hiding.

This time it was behind his house in an open field. The owner kept potatoes in the bunker, with cabbage and other items for the winter. Every night he brought us food, trying to be cautious in order to avoid suspicion. Though he was married with six children, we never met his family.

I recall a Sunday night in late September 1944. Pietrek brought us some food. Because more troops were coming in it was getting very dangerous, and we were so on edge we could hardly eat. The bunker had a little hole that was our exit, and it was covered with dirt and bushes. It was small, but we didn't care since we were safe. We could save our souls a little longer.

On a Thursday evening in early October, Pietrek told us that it was becoming too hazardous. He was afraid the Nazis would invade his house and grounds and find us. Again, we would have to move. We felt the end approaching, and that we would be slaughtered by Nazi bullets.

That night we went into the woods and separated, hiding on the ground under small branches; we could not see or talk to each other. At a distance we heard German voices, the movement of artillery and tanks, and the jangling of other equipment. On the second night the man came back and whispered that he would look for another place for us. He would return the next night at the same time to let us know what he had found.

Yet another day we lay on the ground among the bushes without any food. I ate leaves to stay alive. It was cold and rainy and I was cold, wet, and miserable. Now I wished I had stayed with my parents and put an end to all this misery. I was in complete despair; my life seemed worthless. At nightfall we waited and waited, and finally the signal came—one whistle. Mr. Kawalsky had had a hard time finding us; we came out to meet him, crying, wet, stiff, sick, and anguished.

"I've found you a place," he whispered. "We'll have to move quickly because it's late."

We walked hurriedly through the rustling leaves, trying to be extra careful. Water soaked my shoes and I was ready to give up. My brother took my hand and walked beside me and finally carried me after I fell behind. Our trip took two long hours; we had to be extra careful because of the neighbors and the military guards in the area.

At long last we reached our destination and found the owner waiting. It was early Friday morning. He took us to a bunker in a field about a quarter of a mile from his house. It had been used for storing vegetables from his farm. He had cleaned it out and laid down fresh straw, and he gave us blankets. Oh, how wonderful it was to snuggle down in a dry, warm place! He brought us bread and water once a day. Happy for his help, we paid him with golden dollars and diamonds.

On Sunday night when Andrey brought our food, he told us that his family was afraid to keep us. It was too perilous. Once again we felt we were facing the end. Hardened by terror, we had no more tears to weep and hardly cared what might happen next. We felt like worms crawling on the ground; we could be stepped on at any moment. We knew that the Germans often rewarded the Polish farmers for informing on Jews.

That Saturday, Sunday, and Monday were days of mourning. We didn't eat; we praised one another; we talked; we were convinced that our lives were coming to an end. Yet, hope still crept into our hearts. As the Hebrew proverb says, "As long as the soul remained in us, we still have hope."

On a Monday evening in October 1944, Andrey came to us and said, "You must leave here, but first let Mr. Beinsh go out and look for another place. The rest of you can stay until he returns." We suggested that Peretz go with him, but the man shook his head. "It would be too dangerous for the two of you to go." We had to agree.

He left and said he would see us tomorrow.

CHAPTER VIII

Betrayal

It was a beautiful moonlit October night when our friend went off to look for another hiding place. Within half an hour we sprang to our feet at the sound of a truck and motorcycles drawing near. We stared at each other, speechless and terrified. We heard footsteps and German voices coming closer. Then we heard the bushes being torn from our hiding place.

A loud speaker shouted, *"Juden arouse! Juden arouse!"*—"Jews, come out!" We didn't move.

A machine gun sputtered and shots tore into the bunker; but we weren't hurt, and no one stirred to leave. Then the Germans threw a hand grenade into the bunker. It fell on my upper right thigh but didn't explode because it landed softly.

My brother looked at us and said, "Now is the time to jump and fight!"

I could see in his eyes that he knew he would not survive, that he wanted to die fighting like a hero against the Nazis. He jumped out with his rifle and fired several shots, some soldiers fell before he himself was shot.

Next my sister jumped out with a pistol and fired twice before she fell to the ground.

Then came the Polish officer, holding his rifle, which was covered by a white T-shirt to surrender. The Germans caught him and chained him up.

I was the youngest and the smallest. I jumped out with pistol in hand, but they caught me before I could fire a shot. I stared wildly at the scenery on that beautiful, yet terrible night, seeing everything in the light of the full moon.

What I saw was indescribable. My brother lay on one side, my sister on the other. The Polish officer was chained and I was standing half naked with one

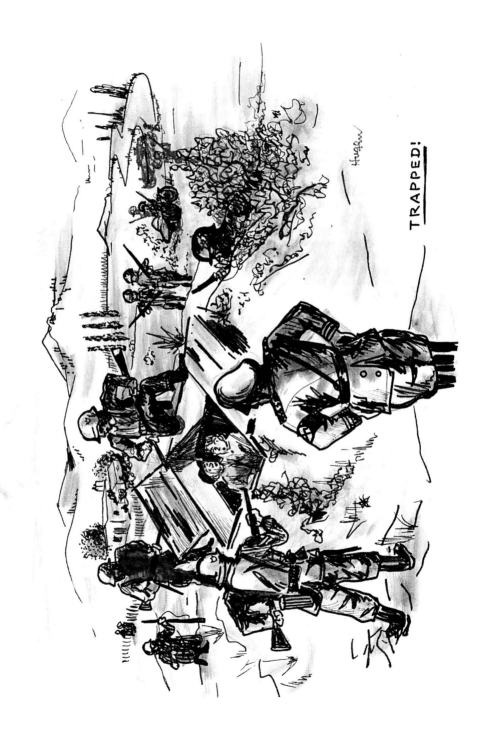

TRAPPED!

German holding a machine gun to my forehead and another holding a gun to the back of my head. I stood still for a half an hour until they finished searching the bunker.

They found little—a couple more rifles, a pistol, personal things, and money. Then I saw the man who had hidden us there. He was wearing a German uniform and thought we would not recognize him.

I called his name. He turned around and looked at me without a word. Was there shame in his eyes?

The Germans unchained the officer and me, and made us lift my sister and brother into a horse-drawn buggy. I could see my sister's blue eyes shining like diamonds in the moonlight, and the back of her head blown away. We found my brother still alive, but limp, pretending to be dead. He hoped they would leave him there on the ground so he could save himself later, but the outcome was tragic.

He was wounded in both legs and could not walk; he was in terrible pain. When we picked him up, he whispered, "You know who gave us away. Look at him, standing there in a German uniform thinking he would not recognize him. Who knows who will survive, but remember what you saw." He wept all the way during the rough ride on the wagon, helpless and in agony. We walked in chains behind the wagon for two and a half hours, finally reaching Nazi headquarters in a little town called Zabne.

When they unchained us I was almost numb; I didn't think I would live through it. Then we had to unload my brother and sister. We placed my sister in front of the building and covered her with a blanket. Then, since my brother couldn't walk, we had to carry him down to the basement. Later the Nazis threw us down there too. By then it must have been ten at night.

Fifteen minutes later, we heard the door being unlocked. Men came in with a flashlight and shouted at my brother, "Get up, fast, fast, up, up!" On hands and knees, he tried to crawl up the stairs. He tried to go fast; then we heard a loud cry from him, and then it stopped. The Germans took him by his hands and feet and threw him down the concrete stairs like a sack of potatoes.

There was nothing I could do for him except talk to him. He could hear, but he shook his head. Next, they took the Polish officer upstairs. It was a short interview, perhaps ten minutes, and I heard the same cries. I knew I would be next. I tried to find out from my brother what questions they had asked, what happened, but he could barely speak.

They hurled our friend down the stairs, unconscious. When he recovered consciousness, he gasped, "Say you don't know." I was shaking but there was nothing I could do. In the dark I could see nothing. Finally the Germans came down with a flashlight and I could see my brother, still bleeding, and our friend, in pain. They cried impatiently to me, "Up, up, quick, quick!"

With much effort I climbed up with them and was taken to another room. Through blurred eyes I saw the officers who interrogated me.

"Are you Jewish?"

THE TORTURE

"Yes."

"Are you Jewish Partisans?"

"No!"

They stretched me out on a long bench and two officers with rubber crowbars beat me on the back.

"Are you a Jewish Partisan?"

"No!"

They hit me until I fainted and fell off the bench.

On all fours I pulled myself to the top of the bench. I could scarcely see.

"Do you know more Jews in this area?"

"No."

"Do you know more Jewish Russian Partisans?"

"No!"

They were drinking and beating me, and when I fainted again, they poured water over me. I could not see, I could not cry out, and I lost my voice completely. I was totally out; there was nothing left of me. I didn't know who I was.

It would be a terrible experience to go through at anytime, but especially so for a boy at fourteen. After the interview they made me sign papers saying I was a Jewish Russian Partisan. By then I didn't care, I was just glad it was over. They threw me down into the cellar again and I landed half dead, not aware of anything.

Later I began to recover and look for my brother. I knew he was in pain and tried to reach him and comfort him. I talked to him, but could hardly understand what he was saying. I heard heavy steps coming down the stairs, and then a blinking flashlight came close. I was afraid and moved away from my brother.

The man walked right in and we all grew quiet, listening to see what he would do. With the flashlight he searched and found my brother on the floor and shined the light straight at him. My brother looked back without fear, as if to say, "I am ready to be sacrificed in the name of G-d."

The SS man, to my horror, took out his pistol, aimed straight at my brother's face and shot him. The moment he walked out, I ran to my brother and found him still alive. The bullet had entered his mouth, knocking out all his teeth, and he was bleeding to death.

I could only understand one word he mumbled: *"Nekuma."* It was the Hebrew word for revenge.

My brother, Peretz, would have been better off dead since he was suffering so. My friend and I were both hurt and we could hardly move, but we tried to help him. We were sitting in a pool of his blood, but there was nothing we could do. It was his turn to die. Tomorrow, we expected, would be ours. We did not expect to get out alive.

While we talked and held each other, we heard steps coming down the stairs. We lay down and my brother wept quietly, knowing these were the final minutes of his life. He knew that when the flashlight shined upon him again, it would be the end.

Peretz had all this time carried a brown sweater with him, a memento of our happier days with the family in Nowy Korczyn. They took that sweater away from him, and covered his face with it so that he would not see the murderer take another shot.

The executioner opened the door and came in, flashed his light at my brother, aimed his gun, and shot him again. He turned and walked out at exactly 3:00 A.M. My brother's heart was beating; he was snoring hard. By morning he was dead.

As I wept and cried for my brother and my sister, I wondered who would weep for me.

The morning was beautiful with a bright shining sun in the sky. Yesterday they were killed and today would be my turn and that of our friend. We talked together.

"My life is over," he said grimly. "I have lost everything, my wife, and my six children. What future is there for me?"

But how young I was and without a chance to live, unable to bear witness to what I had seen and lived through. I wanted to live, even though my friend had given up the fight. However, there was no one to encourage me to fight for survival. Since the day the Germans invaded Poland, I had longed to fight them. I had never given up looking for a brighter tomorrow.

As a believer in G-d and Judaism, I always wondered why we were being punished. What had we done especially the infants and small children?

I lay in that dark little basement next to my brother, with my hands and clothes steeped in his blood. I shivered for lack of clothing and wished sometimes to be with him in death. I cried out, "G-d where are You? Isn't it enough that I've lost my parents, my brothers, and sisters?" There were four stone walls and a concrete floor. There was a small window with iron bars, and outside we could see SS men with machine guns marching past. Our entrance was locked with an iron gate. At 10:00 A.M. we heard steps on the stairs and became rigid. The men unlocked the iron gate to the basement.

"Come out now, but you have to bring the dead body upstairs."

It took all our strength to carry Peretz upstairs and lay him down on the floor next to my sister. Seeing them like that, lying face to face, unseeing, dead, I stared at them, like a stone, unable to move.

Someone hit me on the head with a rifle and I screamed, "G-d, where are You? Take me with them; don't leave me here alone! I want to be with them!"

The men ordered us to carry the bodies to the horse-drawn wagon waiting for us in front of the office. Six men with machine guns stood there watching.

It was a beautiful sunny day. I had no shoes. I was wearing only a pair of pants and a shirt, but I was strong and hard as a rock. I looked at the sky, the trees, and the birds, and thought how wonderful it would be if only I could fly free like a bird.

Chained to the wagon, we trudged through the cobbled streets to the outskirts of the village, then to a farm where there were three big, leafless trees, swaying in a light breeze. A glorious day for whom?

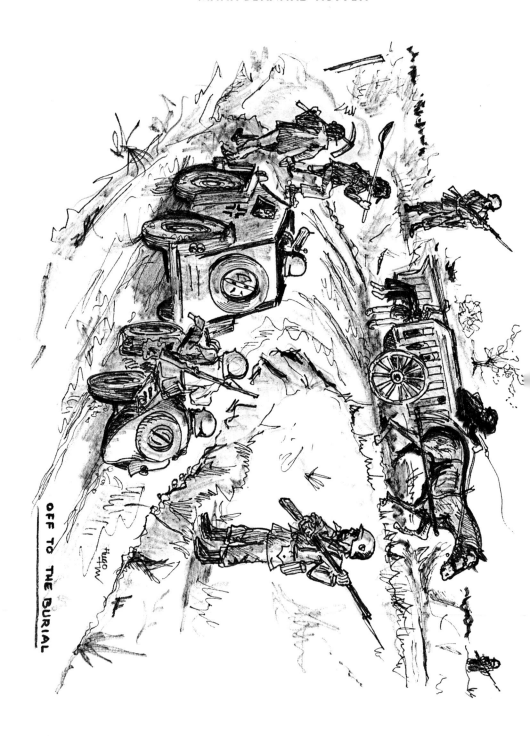

OFF TO THE BURIAL

"G-d," I cried out inwardly, "Behold Your children, the Chosen Ones. Here we will be buried like animals and no one will know about us, only You. You are the only one who can save me, that I might tell our story to the world!"

The Germans came over and ordered us to remove the bodies from the wagon. Then four of the men left to return to headquarters. I looked at my brother and sister and fell upon their bodies. "This is the last time I will see you, dead, with no one to talk to, no one to remember the time we were alive together. This is the last time, like a nightmare, but a true story."

The two remaining Germans prodded us, and my friend and I took shovels from the wagon and began to dig the grave. To my friend I said, "I am afraid, and I have a strange feeling about not knowing what might happen next."

He replied impassionately, "I have nothing to live for." Then I recalled his family was gone, his wife and six children.

When I asked if there was some way to escape, he said, "My child, with these machine guns aimed at us, you will never be able to get away from them."

I was shivering. *No one can help me,* I thought. I prayed silently to G-d: *If there is a G-d, show me a miracle so that I can survive as a witness.* The grass was turning yellow and it was wet with dew. I looked at the two remaining SS men and wanted to kill them both. While we were digging, I muttered to my friend, "Let's kill them with our shovels. You knock one over the head and I'll kill the other one. Then we'll take the machine guns and run."

"It's impossible," he muttered back. "Nothing doing." The grave grew bigger, large enough for six people. I was tired. I said to the SS man, "I can't dig anymore. Do whatever you have to with us."

One of them looked at me. "How old are you?"

"Fifteen," I answered.

"You have a whole life ahead of you and no chance to survive," he replied.

He ordered us to take down the bodies from the wagon and place them in the grave. It was this last image of my brother and sister, dead, not alive, that stays fixed in my mind's eye. In the grave their open eyes stared back at me.

"It just can't be," I wailed. I wept as I closed their eyes and covered them with a blanket and my brother's sweater. I recited the memorial prayer, the *Kaddish*, and again fell upon their bodies. My friend picked me up and pulled me out of the grave.

"Now them," he said quietly. "Later it will be us, and there will be no one to say Kaddish for us."

We covered their bodies with earth and bade them farewell, forever.

As we drove back to the railroad station at Domberowa, an area rich in gas and oil, we could hear the Russian artillery in the distance.

While traveling I murmured to my friend, "We've both lost our loved ones, but no matter what we have been through, the will to live is still strong in us." I reminded him of the time we had shared, of what we had suffered together. "We must live to tell our story to the generations to come," I said.

I heard cannon fire and my friend said to me in Polish, "The Russians cannot be far away."

How I longed to run, to save my life and bear witness to everything that had happened. No one had tried to save us. Someone must have known that millions of us were being tortured and killed, and yet few were saying anything. It seemed as if the whole world looked on and was silent. At that moment it seemed as if G-d were looking upon His chosen children in silence as well.

When we arrived, the men unchained us and locked us up in the jail.

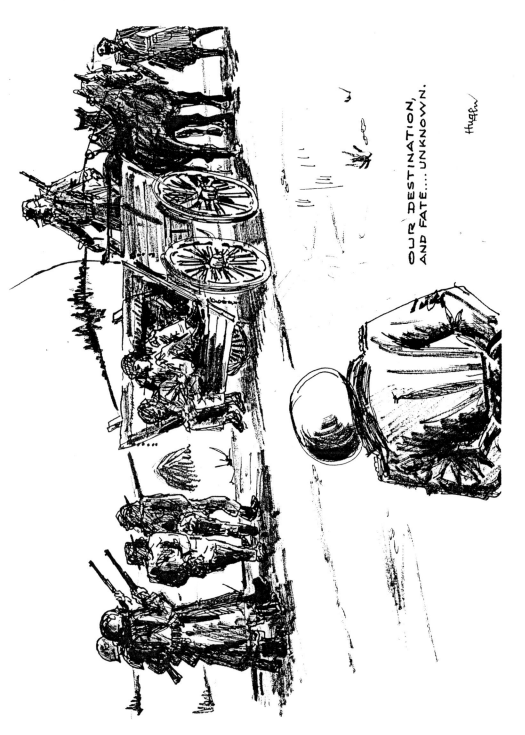

CHAPTER IX

Who Will Say Kaddish for Us?

All that night in the jail we lay shivering and shuttered at every noise. *No, not yet, not yet. G-d,* I said in prayer, *give us a little more time.*

We could trust only in G-d; there was no one else to help us. "We are in your hands and we trust in you. You can save us and guide us through our faith in you."

It was a long, cold, frustrating, and terrifying night. In the morning they tied our hands and took us away. We rode in a wagon with four SS men. We were not permitted to speak or ask any questions; we had no idea where we were being taken. We could only look around at the beauty of the countryside and hope for life.

We heard the sounds of a battle nearby machine guns, artillery, and exploding bombs. Our only consolation was knowing that death would bring us the tranquility we longed for.

The Bible tells us that with faith, G-d prolongs life somehow. My faith grew stronger as we traveled that day. From afar we saw an oil and petroleum refinery, and it reminded me of the city of Moshciza. My father used to say that those were the factories that supplied petroleum for our kerosene lamps. We didn't have electricity then.

As we traveled toward the city, we saw more and more tanks, armored vehicles, and infantry. Scared, we hid our heads and prayed to arrive soon at our destination. As we drove through the streets, we heard the men saying that the Russians were moving west and would be here in a few days. Maybe that was good and maybe not. Finally, we arrived at SS headquarters and the men there took charge of us.

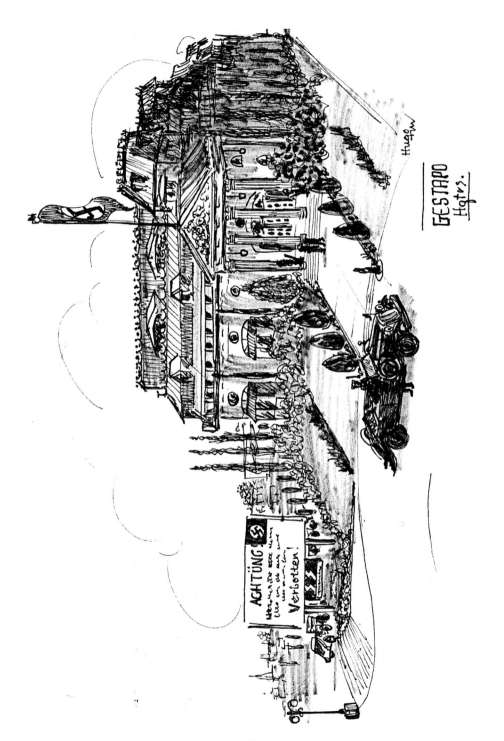

We were locked up in jail overnight. Then we were questioned together. Why were we hiding? What contact did we have with the underground? How did we get guns and from whom? Did the Russians supply us with arms? I would not have answered the questions even if I could. Then they took us to separate rooms and questioned us some more. I told them I did not know anyone in the underground and we were by ourselves just trying to survive the war.

Obviously, they said, we were against the German government and therefore had to be punished. We were beaten with rubber sticks, iron bars, and anything else at hand. I couldn't see or talk, and at last signed documents confessing to whatever they wanted.

They threw me back into the cellar. At night they brought me up to the office. There was an older man with the SS leaders; I could see the hate in his eyes when he walked in—hate for the Jews and especially for the underground.

"Why are you hiding?"

I answered, "I am very young and I don't want to die."

"Are you underground?"

"Yes."

"How long?"

"Since I ran from the ghetto."

"Why did you run from the ghetto?"

"Because so many people were dying from starvation, hard labor, and beatings."

"What made you think you could survive here?"

"Give me the chance," I cried, "and I'll survive!"

The tall gray haired man continued to question me. He looked at me hard. "How can you prove you're Jewish?"

"That's easy," I answered. "I'm circumcised. I speak and read Hebrew. I speak Yiddish. I know all the holidays and I can pray. I ran away from the ghetto because I'm Jewish. I left the underground to save my life because I'm Jewish."

He stood towering over me, because he was quite tall and I was a small boy. "Show me. Prove you are circumcised," he commanded. Angrily, I unbuttoned my pants and let them down so he could see.

"Yes, you are Jewish. We caught you fighting our SS men and the German government."

In desperation I cried, "I wasn't fighting. I was trying to save my life because I am young and want to live!"

I was fifteen years old and eager to live. How could an old wrinkled man who has already lived his life kill me? There was no justification for this. "G-d where are You? Wasn't it enough that I lost my family? That punishment should be enough," I cried.

"Why are you crying?" the man asked. "It's only going to hurt for a moment, then everything will be over."

I asked, "What kind of death will you give me?"

PROVING TO BE JEWISH, AND CHOICE OF DEATH.

He looked at me with his cold evil eyes and said, "What do you prefer? A bullet in your forehead, a bullet in the back of your head, or to be hung?"

I told him that it made no difference. "Kill me the easiest way possible so that I won't have to suffer like my brother did." I wanted them to get it over with so that I could be together with my family and friends. I felt better and did not fear death. G-d would decide my destiny.

He told me that tomorrow would be the day, but there was no set time. This ended the interview.

I cried all night long; the only thing on my mind was not to suffer like my beloved brother, but to die like my sister with a smile on her face and her beautiful eyes wide open. An SS man told us that in the morning we would leave.

That night from the cell we heard artillery and gunfire. We hoped the Russians would arrive soon, the faster the better. However, we all know that when you pray for something it doesn't happen right away. It takes time.

The next morning they took us out and again we thought it was the end. It was a cold morning, dark and cloudy, with snow flurries. We hardly cared. It was miserable, but we figured that a few minutes more would not matter. They tied our hands, put us into a motor vehicle and said we were going for a ride. It would not be a joy ride for us.

We drove for nearly two hours, passing military installations, tanks, armored cars, and other military equipment. In town the traffic was heavy with soldiers and civilians. Things looked normal for the moment. Finally, we came to a street that was surrounded by the military. We were driven through the gates of an office, where they told us to get out.

We were in Tarnow, which had been a nice city with a large Jewish population. Were any of them left now? We hoped to find someone to talk to.

The Germans escorted us to the military office. They told us their records indicated we were Jewish Partisans. We said yes, it was true. Then they put us in a military jail by ourselves.

For several weeks they questioned us about other Jewish people and partisans. Each time I walked out black and blue, half dead, not knowing my name or who I was. The last interrogation was by an SS officer; I will never forget it. I fainted several times. They revived me with cold water. Then they tried to kill me by suffocating me with a gas mask, putting it over my face and closing the tube so that no air could get in. They sat on my stomach to make sure I would die.

I stopped breathing, but I heard one SS man ask the other if I were still alive.

"No. He's dead," he assured the other officer.

The man took the mask off and I revived, gasping for breath. I didn't know what was going on around me. I could not see but I heard them say, "He's alive, he's alive! Darn you, darn you!"

They spoke in German. They carried me on a stretcher down to my cell and threw me on the floor like a piece of wood. I lay on the floor for hours and didn't know if I was dead or alive. I can only remember that my friend came to talk to me.

TORTURE WITH
A GAS MASK

"Thank G-d you're alive, you are alive," he whispered. For two days he fed me bread and water to sustain me.

After several days I woke up and remembered everything that had happened to me. I begged G-d to give me strength, to save me, and give me the courage to tell my story to the world. Although I was only fifteen, somehow G-d gave me the strength to withstand all the punishment and torture. Day in, day out, there were beatings. Often I asked for death, but it did not come.

Everyday that fall of 1944, we heard planes roaring overhead, dropping bombs throughout the city of Tarnow. I scarcely cared what was happening because of the beatings I suffered. Then one day an SS man told us, "Tomorrow you are leaving here." We did not ask any questions.

We didn't sleep that night wondering how many hours that we had left to live; only G-d knew. We prayed and embraced each other. It was winter, there was snow on the ground, and we had very little clothing; we were freezing. We were without shoes and had to walk to the trucks in the snow. We cried out but no one would help us. We looked up to the heavens and asked how long this punishment and suffering would continue.

I cried, "Don't let me suffer. I just want to be with my parents, brothers, and sisters." But again I survived and the suffering went on.

We stood at the train station for four hours waiting for the train to arrive. My feet were freezing in the snow, but I finally found a newspaper to put under them. Then we were packed into a car, guarded by soldiers with machine guns, and the train chugged off. Again we didn't know our destination.

In about an hour the train was bombed. Several compartments were hit by Russian planes. We were stranded for hours while they fixed the track. Ambulances and trucks arrived to take the dead and wounded off the train. Thank G-d our compartment was spared.

The next day we arrived in the city of Krakow, one of the largest cities in Poland. Near the city was a labor camp called Plashauw. The Germans gave us coffee but no food while they kept us in the train for twenty-four hours. In any case, we were too concerned about our fate to eat anyhow.

The next day we were loaded onto trucks. I wanted to jump but was held back by an SS man holding a machine gun to my head. There was nowhere to run anyway; behind us were trucks and motorcycles with guards. Now filled with terror, I prayed to G-d to spare my life.

Finally we arrived at the gates of Montelupe, the largest jail in Poland. I had heard of it as a child, heard that no one comes out of it alive. I was really scared. When my name was called, I was speechless. G-d had not heard our plea; more suffering lay ahead! How long, O Lord, how long must I suffer? "Please save at least one member of the Kupfer family," I begged.

There was tight security as we marched through the gates, guarded by SS men. There were about a hundred of us, Jews from different countries. As we walked toward the building, we saw Jewish workers. We couldn't stop to talk, but on the

PROBABLY THE LAST STEPS OF OUR LIVES.

way I asked where we were going. In Yiddish, they replied, "We can't tell you." One said, "You're going to take a shower."

That terrified us because we'd heard how Jews were herded into buildings supposedly "to take a shower" but were gassed instead.

I was handed a towel as I walked to the shower room. I then began to utter words from the morning prayer, "Save me, Oh Lord our G-d, the Lord is One," and entered the shower room no longer afraid. We actually took a shower and the Germans gave us clothing to put on.

There were four of us in a cell; I at fifteen was the youngest. It was December 1944. Each morning the Germans checked the cell. We had two meals a day: black coffee and a slice of bread for breakfast, and a cup of soup and a slice of bread at night. We had no idea how long we would be there and thanked G-d for the gift of each day.

A rabbi named Moskovitcz came to our cell one morning. He prayed for us in Hebrew and translated it into German. "May the Lord bless and guard you; may the Lord grant you peace." He asked us which country we came from. I saw that he too was frightened. His face was pale, and he seemed afraid of his own shadow. He said *shalom* and left with the guards. We knew that any day now the Germans would come for us again. Our lives were completely in G-d's hands.

On Monday night they told us that we would be shipped out the next morning. As usual we knew nothing about our destination. The rabbi came to bless us. Yet, strangely enough, we stayed on there for three more weeks. Every Friday the rabbi brought us a little wine and a piece of challah.

On a nice, sunny, but cold, day they loaded us again on three trucks, about twenty-five people to a truck. There were guards on the trucks and behind us were motorcycle guards. I wanted to leap from the truck but the guards stopped me. We drove through Krakow for two hours.

Finally the trucks stopped at a labor camp, and I saw the name "Plaszow." The gates were opened and the trucks drove in. Each camp had an Appellplatz: a parade ground used as a counting place. We stood there for about two hours. Finally some Jewish people passed by and muttered in Polish, "No good"—*"Nie dobzie, nie dobzie."*

About 2:00 P.M. the SS men arrived. Among them was Lager-fuehrer, the camp commandant. We stood face to face with him while he looked at us. Then the selection process started, with prisoners directed either to the left or to the right. My common sense told me I should hope to go where there were fewer inmates, but the SS men directed me to the larger group.

I didn't want to go there and thus was beaten with a machine gun and a rifle until blood ran over my face and clothing. As I lay on the ground, the men stepped all over me with their boots until I was more dead than alive.

They picked me up and carried me to the SS general and the camp president named Berkovitch. The latter asked, "Would you like to work for us?" In German I answered that it would be a pleasure to work for him. He led me off to join the

smaller group of inmates. President Berkovitch took the group to the barracks and then sent me to the hospital a block away. The doctor looked at me and murmured, "You are lucky, you are very lucky." He cleaned and bandaged my wounds and then said he'd try to get me a job working for him in the hospital, and he did.

A few days later my wounds were healed and I was working in the hospital, cleaning and helping the sick, and cooking for them. I worked all over the hospital. One morning I went out to get some heating coal from the store. While I was putting coals in the pails, the SS men walked in and saw me. They sent dogs after me, threw me on the floor, and dragged me around the Appellplatz. I was crying and covered with blood. The Nazi guards just laughed.

The doctor ran out and asked the guards for permission to take me in. I told him the story and he warned me that the best time to go for coal was in the morning. We never knew when the Germans would appear, and we had to be on the alert at all times. This Dr. Krulewicz was a very nice man. He spoke Polish, German, and Yiddish.

I worked in the hospital until the end of December 1944 when the final march from Plaszow began. There were at least eight hundred of us Jews marching in groups of two hundred. We were forced to leave because the Russians were coming.

We marched through the streets of the beautiful city of Krakow. It was wonderful to see something outside the labor camp. Some Poles shouted at us, *"Zidie do Palestine!"*—"Jews to Israel!" Some marchers managed to escape and ran through the streets, but whether they reached safety I did not know.

We marched on for days. I kept hoping that the Russians would overtake and save us; that was a dream. We marched to the gates of Auschwitz. We stayed in barracks there for a week. I was housed with other minors.

The camp was surrounded by electronic fences guarded by Nazi SS. My job in Auschwitz was cleaning the streets and loading the dead into the wagons. Thousands of people died from starvation, a horrible sight for a teenager to witness.

In Auschwitz we were given soup and a slice of bread for lunch. The soup was so thin it was transparent. At night we had black coffee and, because we were minors, another slice of bread. Often I went to sleep hungry because I kept my slices of bread to eat the next morning. I had to keep them in my pocket so no one could steal them. In the morning I ate the bread with water, which gave me enough strength to be able to go to work.

We slept on bunks, four to a bed. Weighing eighty-five or ninety pounds, no one was fat enough to take up much room. One night they told us we would get nothing to eat but would have breakfast in the morning. Once again we were moving; no one knew where or why. All I could do was pray for my health so that I would be able to work, walk, and maybe have a chance to survive until the war was over. It was now January 1945.

The next morning we marched to the train which would take us from Auschwitz to nowhere. Many could not make it to the train and were sent back by truck or shot on the highway. How relieved we were after that long march to see the train. Most of our group was between twelve and eighteen years of age. They packed us in like sardines. There were twenty-five or thirty boxcars and each held forty-five to fifty persons.

We waited for several hours before the train left. There was a tiny window for air, but only enough for a few hours. Some boys had to go to the bathroom but there were no facilities; the whole car became a bathroom. Some died. The SS men gave us permission to go to the bathroom when the train stopped during the night.

On the second day we reached Czechoslovakia. Some boys spoke the language and the Czechs were very kind. They brought us food, apples and pears, and though the Germans did not allow them to give it to us, we did manage to get something to eat. The Germans gave us only one meal a day.

On the third day the train was bombed and several compartments were badly damaged; several people were killed. We ran from the train. I lay on the ground and did not move. The planes were American. We stayed in the field for one day while they fixed the train, enjoying fresh air at last.

The train was heading for another death camp, Mauthausen, in Austria, a camp we had not heard of. As we were loaded onto trucks heading for the camp, American planes flew over again, and we had to seek shelter. It was no picnic, but we hoped to survive by obeying their rules.

The next day we entered the camp. There were prisoners and workers of all nationalities speaking a multitude of languages. They wore striped suits with a Mogen David Star. I was put in with the minors, and the next day I registered at the camp office. They asked me all kinds of questions because my records accompanied me there.

We were ordered to take a shower and were told we would get new clothes. Once again we entered with trepidation, fearing gas. We took a shower; it was water, not gas!

Again we were transferred, spent a week at the new location, and then we were taken out in the middle of the night without notice. At the new place we worked on the highways. Then we were packed into the train for Dachau, spending two days on the train, wondering what would happen to us.

On the third day we began another trip and were bombed, this time by the British. Much blood was spilled in vain, but how could we question G-d? Many nights I hoped I would not wake up having to face another day of suffering.

Now it seemed to me that G-d had kept watch over me and kept me alive despite all the past suffering. I hoped He would save me in the future. My hopes rose and I began to feel better. Day by day I said, "Thank You, G-d." I believed He would continue to be with me, helping me to overcome these horrors until I found freedom once more.

At last we reached the concentration camp at Flossenbürg, and my friends and I were placed in Barrack 23. Some of the boys I saw there were skeletons with not enough strength even to get down from their bunks.

They were beaten up, had ravaged faces, and could not talk. It was a horrible scene. I inhaled some fresh air and told myself this could not last much longer.

Flossenbürg was in the mountains and very cold. Some boys froze to death or died from starvation and hard labor. I forced myself to live with these conditions, to strengthen myself and not give up. We had to get up at 5:00 A.M. and wash with cold water. Rarely did we have hot water. When we took showers in cold water, some boys froze to death. Some were too sick to work. *How many died in bed?* was the question that ran in my mind. How many were killed outside going to work or lining up to be counted? If a single person was missing from the count, the rest had to stay out in the cold until he was found. If the person could not be found, the Germans took boys from the group and shot them in front of us. They warned us that if this happened again, the same thing would be repeated.

We were taken to work in trucks. We worked on railroads, highways, and in factories. We were given an extra piece of bread per day. In the morning there was black coffee with a thin slice of bread; in the evening a bowl of soup and a slice of bread.

Boys killed each other trying to take that slice of bread. I hid mine so that no one would take it from me, but several times I had to fight to hold onto it. Fortunately, I was strong enough to win these fights.

Once, two brothers fought each other for a piece of bread; one killed the other and took his bread. We were like animals. No one cared for anyone else because we knew we would be killed; it was only a matter of time. We would die by bullets, hard labor, or starvation. We could last only a few more days before we died.

We worked day in and day out, and each day there were fewer of us to count. We were eager to live, but we felt like flies cast into graves.

Each day we dug more and more graves, always wondering when our time would come; where would I lie and in what corner, facing up or facing down?

G-d's name was always on my lips and sometimes I could hear Him. Each day, I thought, brought me nearer to survival, hard as it was to believe. The whole world must learn what happened to the young and old, the flesh and blood of our people.

MY LAST CONCENTRATION CAMP. (FLOSSENBERG – 1945.)

CHAPTER X

The Last Treks

How often I pined for the little town where I was born. I wondered if there would ever again be a world at peace, with city streets and buildings cleared of bombs and rubble, with spring landscapes of trees in leaf and lilac bushes in bloom, with people eating and sleeping without worrying if soldiers would burst into their homes. Would I survive to see such a world?

February and March of 1945 passed, and it would almost be spring. We saw the snow melt away from the mountains and watched the birds flying back. The birds' songs reminded me of years gone by in my old home, with its trees, garden, sunflowers, and daisies. I was reminded of my home filled with abundant food, warmth, freshness, cleanliness, and the company of my beloved family. Then I thought of those long periods of inactivity in the bunkers that had become my home. How much longer could I endure this? Only G-d could answer.

By the end of March we heard rumors that we were to leave Flossenbürg. On April 10, orders came to leave the camp. This time there were no trucks or trains; we would march on foot. There were 200 boys in my barrack. We knew very little. I tried to follow orders on the assumption that I might have a better chance to stay alive, regardless of cost in suffering. I counted on my wiry strength and my dream of life in peacetime to carry me through the ordeals.

About four hundred boys from Barracks 22 and 23 were split into groups of eleven each. We marched mostly at night. In the daytime we stayed in fields, woods, or in barns, guarded by SS troops.

Some youngsters were too weak to walk and fell along the highway. No help was given. Once a day we received water and a piece of dried bread; that was all.

DEATH MARCH   APRIL 22, 1945   (I FELL IN A DITCH.)

We were starving, all skin and bones, with eyes bulging from our heads. During that last week we could barely rise to our feet as we stumbled along the road.

By Sunday, April 15, 1945, only fifty-seven were left of the four hundred. Those who died on the march were left on the road or thrown into ditches; we saw animals and birds eating their flesh. This horrible sight can never be erased and will last in my mind's eye until my death.

On that last Sunday we stayed in a farmer's barn and tried to find a way to save ourselves. Some boys dug themselves under the straw and awaited our departure. Two of my friends begged me to join them, but I refused. I had decided that what was going to happen to the rest of us was going to happen to me too.

That Monday the SS called us out and counted us. Five boys were missing. The SS searched the barn and found them. They lined them up and told them to run, and then gunned them down in flight. Their bodies were thrown into the fields. By this time we were so used to such horrors that it meant nothing to us.

But the memories remain to this day, still inflicting suffering. Now there were only fifty-two boys left.

The guards told us we were on a death march—they could not use bullets on us; we were left to die of starvation. Wednesday they gave us one piece of bread and water, while they lunched on chicken. They threw the bones into the field; some boys ran for them and were gunned down. I never ran after anything, never volunteered, never did anything that could cause me more pain. G-d gave me the vision of this passive resistance, the will not to do anything that wasn't absolutely necessary. He guided me so I might live to tell this story to the world. G-d gave me the strength to withstand terrors and hardships. Now there were three SS men instead of six guarding us.

To Jews the number eighteen is a lucky number that signifies life. On Wednesday, April 18, 1945, I told myself that G-d would restore my life and strength and redeem me from suffering and death. It was my faith that kept me alive.

But on Thursday and Friday I felt my strength waning. I knew it was Friday night and it reminded me of my home and my family. I wanted desperately to be able to survive and memorialize their names.

On Saturday we reached the outskirts of an unknown town and began to hear bombing. The sound of artillery grew louder and louder. We spent that night at a farm; now there were only thirty-six of us left. We heard the lady from the house talking to the SS men, telling them the Americans were near. While we stayed in the barn that Sunday, we heard military equipment on the highway and the sounds of tanks and machine guns. We wondered how far away the Americans were.

The SS woke us up in the middle of the night to leave again. Early that morning, April 23, 1945, we were dragged for miles through what looked like No Man's Land until I could walk no farther. The SS men disappeared into the woods. I fell into a ditch by the roadside and fainted.

Monday I woke up in a hospital. I was frightened and wanted to run out, but some men held me and spoke to me in German. They were Americans, but I was scared of them and afraid to believe what they said. Finally, a chaplain, also speaking in German, convinced me not to be afraid. The Americans were actually here and he himself was a Jew. His name was Chaplain Schwartz.

At last I calmed down. I was skin and bones; they gave me milk, soup, and medicine to restore my strength. Many boys died during the liberation, unable to digest the food given them. For three weeks I stayed in a church that served as an emergency hospital in a city called Nauburg Van Vald. It was surrounded by woods and trees and had a population of about fifty thousand. It was near the Czechoslovakian border.

Slowly I began to recover, to walk and eat, and to feel normal again. I asked for the opportunity to pray and thank G-d for granting us freedom. A chaplain came to conduct services for us each morning. Later the American doctors told me I had been in such weakened condition they did not believe I would recover. It was G-d's miracle that helped me to survive. Three weeks later they sent me to Bad Reichenhal, a convalescent home. As a minor I was placed with other youngsters. Representatives of organizations from all over the world came to visit us. They wanted to find homes for us in their countries: England, America, Australia, and many others.

I didn't wish to leave until I discovered what had happened to my brother Harry and sister Sarah. I didn't know to which concentration camp they had been sent. Everyday I hoped to hear something but never did. Lists of survivors from the camps were available, but I didn't see any of my family on those lists. I didn't know which direction to turn.

Many of my friends registered to get out of Germany because they hated it so much. We all wanted to get out; we were eternally afraid that something else might happen, another catastrophe, even though the Americans were here.

I finally registered to go to England as a minor; there was the possibility for adoption. I wanted to leave and find some happiness while continuing the search for my brother and sister. In spite of the assurances, I was afraid that the Americans would stop looking for them once I had left. I stalled for weeks, until the beginning of 1946. I was supposed to leave with some friends for England the first week in March; everything was arranged.

A young man chanced to come by looking for relatives and he saw my name. He ran to find me because he had a message for me—he knew where my brother and sister were! Finally, they let him talk to me. He gave me the names of Sarah and Hirschel Kupfer. He knew the camp in Poland where they were and the city in which they were born, and I believed him.

Instead of leaving for England, I begged to go visit my brother and sister. The English gave me special permission to travel with a military convoy of two jeeps and four people to the camps at Landsberg and Lech. There were about eight thousand Jews there in the camps.

Finally, we arrived after traveling two days and a night. We asked directions to the office where we could find the lists of survivors. Camp Landsberg was the first camp to be liberated. There we could find lists of survivors from the concentration camps. As I got out of the jeep, I saw a young woman in the distance crossing the plaza. She looked like my sister! I yelled, "Sarah, Sarah, is that you?"

She could hardly believe it was I, her brother Mark! She had heard I had been killed along with my brother and sister. She told me my brother Harry was alive too.

We cried and cried with joy at this reunion after all those dreadful years. We talked until our voices gave out; we simply were unable to speak another word. It took us time just to collect ourselves. Then my brother found out I had come there. He had been working when he heard, and dashed to the office where Sarah and I were still weeping with joy. This reunion went on for hours.

The English agency wanted me to return with them, but I refused to leave my brother and sister, who would not let me out of their sight. It took two days to clear the papers; my brother and sister had to sign responsibility papers and promise to take care of me. The second day the agency made a proposition. Would I come back if my sister came along? I still refused; I wanted us all to be together. They said it could not be done and they left me papers in case I changed my mind. I never wrote them or called them.

I was fifteen and a half and wanted to go back to Poland, but my brother and sister said, "Nothing doing!" I explained what had happened. I had a mission to accomplish, to find the Poles who brought the SS to kill us, so I could take revenge on them. My brother and sister stood guard at all times and wouldn't let me out of their sight. Finally, I got involved in school and organizations and had no time to plan on running to take revenge. I attended a public high school and a vocational school sponsored by the Organization for Rehabilitation Training (ORT).

I wanted to learn a trade in order to support myself in Israel, then called Palestine. One day at school the teachers told us a visitor was coming—General Eisenhower, leader of the American Army which had liberated the camps. We worked hard to clean our school and wore our best clothes for the occasion. We wanted to impress the general.

The next day General Eisenhower and his staff walked into the school, smartly dressed with all his brass and decorations. He looked around and said, "Very nice, very nice." His interpreter told us he liked what we were doing in the machine shop and he liked what we were learning in our school. Then he smiled that broad friendly "Ike" smile, put a hand on my head, and tousled my hair! Shaking my hand, he said, *"Gooten tog schuler"*—"Good day and goodbye students."

That year, 1946, thousand of boys and girls registered to go to Palestine. The trip was illegal, but it was the only place for Jews in search of a permanent home. Before we could leave for Palestine, we had to be physically examined by different organizations; and many who were unable to recover sufficiently from the ordeal of the camps were rejected. My sister Sarah and I spent most of the day taking the physical exam. She was accepted; I was rejected. The doctors said I was too weak for such a dangerous trip, but perhaps in six months I could go. That never happened.

David Ben Gurion, Israel's first prime minister, came to the camp and spoke for over two hours. He talked of the terrible times we had experienced and of our lack of a homeland. He believed we could build a state for ourselves and for our children. It would not be easy, he told us, but if we all worked together, G-d would help us and we would be successful. That was the essence of his speech.

We yearned to go to Eretz Yisrael, our homeland, and a dream of our people for two thousand years. Young and old alike believed we would live in the land of our forefathers. Ben Gurion kindled the same enthusiasm in the other camps where he spoke. Many of my friends and schoolmates had already left illegally. By now, thousands more had registered to leave. We knew what the hardship of this trip might be, but no one cared because we were at last going home. That was the only way to Eretz Yisrael.

Leaders of different organizations helped me to make plans. I belonged to Mizrachi and was one of the leaders of the B'nai Akiba, the children of Rabbi Akiba. For days and weeks I spoke to other youngsters and told them the dangers we might encounter and the uncertainty of what lay ahead of us. We knew we would have to travel great distances on foot through strange countries about which we knew little.

My sister left with one group. They marched day and night, and it took months before they reached the shore and crossed the sea into Palestine. For weeks and months we heard nothing from our sister, but we supposed that everything was fine. The pilgrims, both young and old, were dedicated, knowing whatever they suffered now would mean future generations would have a land to call their own in Eretz Yisrael. Finally, we heard good news.

Sarah wrote that her group had reached Milan, Italy. In that large industrial city they were recruiting other youngsters to leave with them. They had to wait for further instructions before they could continue their journey.

Then, at the appointed time, they left under cover of darkness; the guides knew the way to the sea and used no lights. They paid people who took them to the awaiting ship.

Many ships had sailed to Israel without hindrance, but my sister was on the renowned *Exodus*, which was captured by the British. The passengers went on strike and didn't eat or drink. For days they debated how to continue resisting their captors. Unfortunately, too many were seasick and starving and had to give up. The British escorted them to Cypress and placed them in still another camp. Jewish people all over the world denounced the action of the British in waylaying of the *Exodus*. Needless to say, the internees were bitter. Those who had survived concentration camps, with their barbed wire and sadistic guards, had had enough of this kind of treatment. But at least in Cypress they were not in mortal danger and were not tortured; they were fed and not treated unkindly.

As much as I hated Germany, I decided to remain until Sarah's group was released from the camps. Meanwhile I attended an ORT technical school and learned to be a tool and die maker. I also attended a gymnasium, or high school, in Munich, Germany, and ran the Jewish youth organization to which I belonged.

I finished school and still wanted to go to Eretz Yisrael, but again I was rejected because of my health. In 1947 I decided I simply had to leave Germany. None of us could rid ourselves of the fear of a resurgence of Nazism and persecution. As a minor I had a good chance of emigrating to England, Australia, or Canada, all of which offered a chance of eventual emigration to Israel. I filled out dozens of applications, and after two months, was sent to a camp for minors in Hamburg where I spent my last three months in Europe.

Many of my friends were at that camp, among them Hirsch Leviton and Michael Tag, so it was like a reunion. We had a wonderful time until our departure—what a contrast it was to the nightmare of the concentration and work camps! Even so, when the notice of approval arrived, I wept because I felt I had betrayed the Jewish state and my people. I remembered my brother's words of comfort when he put his arms around me and said, "You did the best you could, Mark. Go to America and you might still end up in Israel."

On April 10, 1946, Michael and I were among the youngsters chosen to sail on the *Mariner Jumper*, an American warship. But on the second day I fell deathly ill and could not eat for almost eight days. The ship sailed by way of Halifax, Nova Scotia. Although I was miserable for days, the American sailors were kind to all of us. We spoke no English and we came from many different countries. There was a constant babble in at least ten languages; Magyar, French, German, Russian, Polish, Yiddish, Hebrew, and Spanish as well as a variety of Slavic and Czech languages.

We managed, chiefly through Yiddish, to talk together. For the first time I heard of the Statue of Liberty, the lady with the torch held high to guide and welcome newcomers. We talked about the tales we'd heard of America, where money was lying on the ground just waiting to be picked up—we actually believed them! None of us had much baggage; I felt lucky to be clothed in long pants and a jacket and to carry a spare shirt and slacks.

For most of the journey I was too seasick to eat; I subsisted mainly on soup and water. When I could, I joined the others in song. These were Hebrew songs we all knew, such as *"Heveinu Shalom Aleichem,"* as well as marching songs. We talked about the holidays we celebrated, and held Sabbath services.

There were ten of us to a room; we ate in the well-supplied cafeteria, a wondrous innovation for most of us. Some of us played cards to while away the time. Two days before we docked at Halifax, I began to feel better, but the March weather included rain and snow. Yet it felt good to touch land in spite of the bitter cold.

From there we sailed for New York City and America. I remember our joy when we first sighted that grand Statue of Liberty. Soon we walked off the boat and registered our names. We were free at last! It was an experience I can never forget. We were in America, the land of the free, and the greatest free society in the West, the land of opportunity. But we did not find money in the streets!

The skyscrapers astonished us; so did the masses of people in the streets. My friend Michael went to stay with an aunt, whose husband owned a factory. I stayed at a hotel on Lafayette Street, sharing a room with another emigrant. By now I could manage a few English phrases, such as: "How are you? " "My name is Mark Kupfer," "Goodbye," "Good night," and "Hello." There were Jews all around me, so Yiddish again became the common language. My friend Hirsch stayed at a hotel in Manhattan, but I was living in Brooklyn.

As a minor I had certain privileges but did not know how to take advantage of them. Some of my friends did, and managed very well. At the beginning I stayed with the organization and received some help and advice. However, I wanted to do things on my own.

Part of the time I worked in a factory, cutting leather for shoes, earning 45 cents an hour. The rest of the time I attended a public school around the corner from the hotel. A teacher named Frankel, who wore a neat little mustache, white shirt, and narrow striped suit, was very kind and taught us English from a book with words and pictures. Equipped with a dictionary, textbooks, and writing tablets, I studied and ate in the hotel.

At synagogue services I met a nice couple named Schupach who lived in a two-family house in Brooklyn. They took an interest in me, and since they had no children, I spent a lot of time with them in their second-floor apartment. The privacy impressed me. They had two bedrooms and a bathroom, not as large as the house of my childhood, but with the great asset of privacy—something I had not known in years. They invited me to many meals and we became good friends; they even spoke of adopting me.

When people from the adoption agency came with papers for me to sign, they insisted that I take the Schupach family name. I refused. I could not give up the Kupfer name, the name of my father and forefathers. No amount of money or promises could persuade me to give up my father's name; as long as I lived I would keep it. That ended relations with the adoption agency, and from that time I did everything on my own. I was making friends and making a new life in the U.S., despite all those horrible wasted years.

CHAPTER XI

Life in America

I eventually moved to Chicago from Brooklyn, New York. While working in Chicago, I saved money to bring my brother Harry over from Germany. It took a lot of time; I had to fill out applications and obtain signatures from family and friends. Exactly two years after my arrival, he came to the U.S. When he arrived in Chicago, I arranged a place for him to stay with family and friends, and he made his life there.

In 1952, I left Chicago for Detroit, Michigan, to attend a theological seminary. It was called Yeshivoth Chachmei Lublin. There I studied to be a rabbi.

I met many young men and some of my old friends who had come with me to the United States. These people included Hirsch Levitan, Chaim Toledano, Jack Margolis, Shlomo Rattenberg and Jack Ginsberg. The rabbis who taught us were Rabbi Moshe Rattenberg, the Dean; Rabbi Hirshberg; Rabbi Frankel; Rabbi Grubner; and Rabbi Warhman.

While in Detroit, I also attended Wayne State University, studying business administration and bookkeeping. My goal, to own my own business, eventually did materialize. But this business venture did not last very long because I had to leave.

While a student, I also was a teacher of Hebrew and Yiddish, giving private lessons. This paid for expenses, such as tuition. During the summer vacation, I worked for Ford Motor Company as a tool and die maker. To add to my income, my extra time was spent peddling dry goods from house to house. I saved money for a station wagon and merchandise. I bought goods wholesale and retailed them for a profit. When I made enough money in the retail business, my friend and I started selling ice cream house to house.

Two years later, in 1954, I decided to open a dry good store on Campbell Street. Even though this store was very profitable, in 1956 I decided to leave again for New York.

I bought a new Chevrolet, packed all my belongings, and said goodbye to my good friends with whom I had spent years studying and learning. I made a special effort to see the rabbis who had given me so much of their time, and the knowledge I would carry with me throughout my life. To this day, we remain in contact with one another.

On my way to New York, I stopped in Cleveland, Pittsburgh, and New Jersey to see friends and family. The trip to New York City took five days.

When I arrived in New York, my friend had rented an apartment at 890 Eastern Parkway. I lived there for a year and a half while working as a draftsman in the engineering department of Brooklyn Thermo Panels. I had a good job and was very happy, but lonely for a home and family.

I met my wife-to-be through a friend from Poland. He had invited me to spend the Sabbath with his family. They told me about their friend and I finally got to meet the young lady.

I went out with her a few months and decided to meet her parents and family. Her name was Rose Eisenberg and she had aunts in New York with whom she was staying. Her parents lived in El Paso, Texas.

I knew about Texas but not El Paso. One morning when I went to work, I told my boss that I met a girl from El Paso. He was familiar with El Paso because he had been stationed there in the army at Ft. Bliss, Texas. He said it was a nice city and I would like it.

I told him that I was going to El Paso to meet her parents. He said that I was a good worker and nice person, and he provided me with a round trip ticket. Of course, this was to make sure that I would return!

Rose and I went to El Paso together. The airport was very small and far away from the city. Her parents picked us up and took me downtown to the Paso Del Norte Hotel. It was December 25, 1956, yet there was no snow or ice. The weather there was glorious compared to the eastern cities. In the morning, the sun woke me up and I couldn't believe what I saw. I said, "This is beautiful, it's heaven on earth."

I walked around and saw a wonderful little city that reminded me of Europe. There was a small park in the center of the town and homes nearby surrounded by the Franklin Mountains.

I fell in love with El Paso. If everything works out, I thought, I then would make El Paso my home. I met her parents and her brother and his family. On Friday night, I walked to Synagogue B'nai Zion, where I met Rabbi Joseph Renov and Cantor Jacob Diatel. I became friendly with them, and at the Shabbat morning service they honored me with an Aliya.

During the course of my conversations with the rabbi, I discovered that he had studied in Chicago with the rabbis that I knew. Thus, we became good friends.

I stayed in El Paso for about a week. I visited downtown El Paso, Ft. Bliss, and White Sands National Monument in nearby New Mexico. I loved watching the trolley cars, the police on horseback, and the flow of people across the international boundary between El Paso and Ciudad Juarez. The people were nice and very polite. It was a slow-moving city with many opportunities. As I walked around town I kept thinking how much it reminded me of my hometown in Poland. Everything was situated as it was there. I tried to visualize where my house would be from where I stood in the park. I decided that it would be where the Kress building stood, except my house in Poland was narrow. I felt comfortable that I could make El Paso my home.

After many conversations, Rose and I became engaged. We planned a spring wedding. I returned to New York and informed my boss that I would be getting married and moving to El Paso. He was not happy about the news, but wished me well. I trained someone to take my place.

On March 1, 1957, I said goodbye to my boss, who had been very good to me; loaded all my belongings in my car; and drove to Chicago to see my brother Harry and the family. I was very proud of him. He was married and had four children, two boys and two girls. The boys studied to be rabbis and were ordained; one of them lives in Jerusalem. He is a Hebrew and English teacher in a high school. The older son has a business and is well off. He is a computer engineer for a firm in New York. I am very proud to have a family like this. Besides them, I have various cousins in business and real estate.

At last it was time to leave Chicago. It was very hard to leave my only family in the U.S. My brother convinced me to sell my year-old car to my cousin because he didn't want me to drive to El Paso alone. "Take the train," he said, "you'll enjoy the scenery."

The trip to El Paso took two days and two nights. Along the way the train stopped in many little towns and villages. I did enjoy the scenery especially the change from green to brown in the Southwest. Finally, I reached my destination and the train stopped at the old railroad station located on San Francisco Street.

It was one week before the wedding and many things had to be done. My brother Harry came for the wedding and stayed in the motel across the street from the B'nai Zion Synagogue. We had rented an apartment nearby on Schuster Street from Mrs. Wechter.

That Friday night and Saturday morning, we attended Shabbat services. Rabbi Renov announced that our wedding would be held on Sunday. It is customary that the groom be given an Aliya. After he is called to the Torah, he chants the Haftorah, an important part of the service.

After the services lunch was served for the guests. Everything was a bit tense, but I looked forward to the day of the wedding with great anticipation. I will not forget this event as long as I live, especially because it came one week before Passover, a very important holiday in the Jewish calendar. Passover signifies the redemption of the Jewish people from slavery to freedom.

Our wedding took place on Sunday, March 24, 1957, at the B'nai Zion Synagogue on Mesa Street, a beautiful house of worship with a very nice congregation. Rabbi Renov and Cantor Diatel officiated at the ceremony. Many people attended the wedding and I saw many new faces. It was most enjoyable.

We left for a honeymoon in Las Vegas, Nevada. It was an interesting place and the shows were beautiful. We stayed there for a week and returned to El Paso to begin a new life together.

When we got back to El Paso, I remained at home until the conclusion of Passover, enjoying the climate. When the holiday was over I looked for work and was hired by Joe Aaronson, a friend of the Eisenberg family who owned Aaronson Brothers Corporation. I met him downtown in a small restaurant called Michael's. Dave Saks conducted the interview. Right off the bat I felt comfortable because he sat there eating. He told me I could start at $18 a week. I turned down his offer. It was 1957, not 1927! My father-in-law was upset because I had turned down a job, albeit a low-paying one. Then Dave Saks called and offered me $22 a week plus a 1-percent commission on sales, but I would have to work on Saturdays (the Jewish Sabbath). I was a very religious man and my in-laws were not. They could not understand my reluctance to work on these terms.

I had trouble with my mother-in-law over this. Finally, with a heavy heart, I agreed to accept their terms. However, I found that my troubles were only just beginning. I noticed one day that David Saks was watching my every move. Finally I had asked my friend Sam Deener if he knew what the problem was. He stated that David Saks did not approve of me not shaving on the Sabbath. I did this for religious reasons, but I was ordered to shave—another indignation.

I was assistant manager for three months and then was promoted to manager of the store in Ysleta, located in the outskirts of El Paso.

This store was not doing well. In fact, there was little business and a lack of competent help. I was hired to get the store back in the "black" as they say. I studied the store and my first suggestion was to get rid of the display windows and extend the store sixty feet in the rear to add more space. I got more merchandise and racks, expanded the store, and got the help I needed. In a few weeks there was a complete change. People came around because we offered good household items at reasonable prices. Things were going well.

Then one day Meyer Aaronson, Joe's brother, drove up to the store and immediately noticed the display windows were gone. This infuriated him because that was what he liked most about the store, and I had taken them out. He stormed into the building demanding to know who gave permission to remove them. He kept shouting this over and over until I talked to him. Joe treated me like a son and let me have a free hand in the store. In spite of how Meyer felt about things, Joe let me run the store my way. Actually, no one had cause to complain; the store's profits increased $125,000 to $500,000 a year. The store remained successful and profitable for ten years.

After these ten years, Joe came to me again. It seemed the man who managed the Parisian store downtown was ill with cancer. He wanted to transfer me to downtown to run it. I refused because I loved the store in Ysleta and had made many friends among the customers. Joe called me into his office; he told me I should take the transfer because it would mean more money and opportunity. That changed my outlook and I quickly accepted.

I liked the challenge of a bigger store and the work that went with it. The Parisian was located in a two-story building with a basement. Given Shoes had a department in the basement. On the first floor were the men's and the children's departments. Ladies wear was upstairs. The store was located downtown and there was a lot of competition.

1967 was a memorable year for me because of the Six-Day War in the State of Israel. One day Joe asked me if I had heard the news from Israel. I said yes, and we should not be worried because the Israelis are very strong and determined and will fight for their country until they win.

In May 1967, when the Six-Day War broke out, the State of Israel had three million Jewish people surrounded by 120 million Arabs. The Israelis had faith in G-d and believed in G-d's promise that the land would be given to the Jewish people. They lost a lot of soldiers and many were wounded, but the war resulted in an overwhelming Israeli victory. Israel is a proud country with many problems that will be overcome.

My sister was one of the first people to settle in Israel after World War II, when it was still Palestine. Life was very difficult for her in the beginning. She and others lived in tents, carried water to their homes, and were afraid for their lives. There were not enough jobs and food was scarce; it was very uncomfortable and unpleasant, to say the least. The worst was having to go miles away for water, carrying it back in pails. But Sarah and her husband worked hard so that their children could have a home. Their efforts were rewarded. In 1948 Palestine became Israel, and almost overnight it seemed she became a country. It was a civilized country—there were police, hospitals, an army, schools, and technology—with a culture cut and molded by sweat and tears. I am proud to say my family was a part of the birth of a new nation that had much at stake and developed into one which is respected.

During all these years, as I grew with the company, so did my family. We had four beautiful children. My eldest son, Dov Emil, was named after my father; my daughter Deborah Renee was named after my mother; and my other two sons are Samuel Paul and Abraham Jacob. Dov Emil's Bar Mitzvah was in 1971. Rabbi Leo Heim and Cantor David Grunberger taught Dov. To my mind, Dov was fantastic and unbelievable.

My only surviving brother, Harry, came from Chicago; and my surviving sister, Sarah, came from Tel Aviv, Israel. How delighted they were to see our first son's Bar Mitzvah, which was held at Congregation B'nai Zion. A reception was held at the Sheraton.

In the ensuing years, we had a Bat Mitzvah for Debby Rene and the B'nai

My brother, sister, and myself at my son's bar mitzvah.

Mitzvot for Sammy Paul and Abie Jack. They all attended Hebrew school, Mesita Elementary School, El Paso High School and, eventually the University of Texas at El Paso. Dov and Debby both received their baccalaureate degrees.

Meanwhile, the Parisian store was doing well. I was able to increase profits from $800,000 to $1.5 million dollars. I worked there for thirteen years. By 1981, Mr. Weiss, the owner of the building, wanted to make some changes. I recommended that he make it into three stores, two to rent and one for himself. He told me to fire the employees and hire new ones. I was upset at his insensitivity and said, "Mr. Weiss today you are the boss, you fire them, begin with me."

That was the final year I worked for someone and also the last year of my marriage to Rose. I left for Chicago to be with my brother. Shortly after, I returned to El Paso to be closer to my children.

I settled in a small house on Gregory Avenue and began working in a store called Bonanza City. I didn't like the store because it was very dirty and smelly! I told the owner that I could not work there. It would take me at least two months just to clean it up and make something out of it.

He wanted the store to get off the ground and gave me two months to get it going. Unfortunately, it was about this time the Mexican peso declined, and most store in El Paso suffered as a result. I offered to take a cut in pay until conditions improved.

After five years there, I left. I was treated badly by the owner's son because I was Jewish. To make matters worse, when sales did improve, they did not keep their word regarding my wages.

From that point on I was in business for myself. All of my children were grown and out of college. Dov Emil graduated with bachelor of arts—art education—all levels with teacher certification, Debby Rene earned a bachelor of social work degree, Sammy Paul studied to be an engineer, but chose retail management for his career, and Abie Jack received a bachelor of arts degree in criminal justice. I opened my own business, bringing in merchandise from Las Vegas and Los Angeles to sell them here. I did very well.

The El Paso Jewish community had a dream to build a memorial to those who died in the concentration camps. Land was donated by the Jewish Community Center, and Mr. Louis Rosenbaum hired an architect. Many in the community donated time and money. Some brought articles to be put on display, as well as pictures and documents. The groundbreaking ceremony took place in 1990. I spoke at the University of Texas at El Paso on the subject of the Holocaust.

In April of 1992 the Holocaust Museum was dedicated. It was one of the most important events that El Paso has ever had. There were many dignitaries, including representatives from Catholic churches and other area churches.

Looking back on my life, being able to tell my story of surviving the Holocaust and the education of my children are my greatest accomplishments. Had I remained in Poland, even without the Holocaust, I would not have had the freedom nor the opportunity afforded me in America. This is the life, then, of the young boy who, in a few short months, was torn from a loving, proud family and dropped into the pit of darkness and horror that was the Nazi Holocaust; and who, through strength and determination, rose into the sunshine.

When I was asked, "Why do you write about the Holocaust? So many have already done so." I answered this way: "There are many books written on the subject, but they will never end as long as there is someone left to tell what they witnessed."

I'm proud to be an American citizen in the land of the free. G-d Bless America!

NOTE: *My father died in 1998. My brothers and I were determined to have his book published to honor his memory as well as to honor his desire to have told his eye-witness account of the horrors of the Holocaust.*

—Debby R. Kupfer

Congratulations to:

The Russian people who fought in the Second World War to save humanity and civilization. We thank the Russian Army for liberating the first concentration camps Maidanek, Auschwitz, and others. We shall remember their sacrifices in finally achieving victory over the Nazis.

Holocaust Survivors.

Survivors talk with Soviet liberators in front of the infirmary. Auschwitz, Poland, February 1945. Sovfoto.

Jewish districts
cut off from
others by
barbed wire.

Transportation was
very difficult
around the ghettos.

Secret teaching
was done despite
the Nazis'
disallowance.

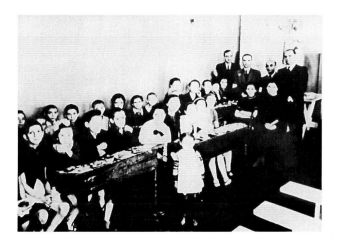

Naked victims awaiting execution.

Warsaw Ghetto Uprising— April 19, 1943. Underground Jews began to resist for the first time.

Ghetto inmate was caught by the Germans later to be killed.

Nazi brutally
cuts off the
beard of a
Jewish man.

Ul. Pawia—Ghetto
in Warsaw, 1941.

Jews arrive at
Warsaw Ghetto
with their
belongings.

Ghetto fighter
leaving bunker
that Germans
had gassed.

Jews who were
captured by the
Germans.

Group of Jews
who were
captured during
the uprising.

The whipping board was another method that the Nazis used to inflict pain on their victims.

Nazis' way of punishing Jewish people without a bullet.

One of the ovens that was used to destroy bodies.

Pile of human ashes taken out of the oven.

American soldiers are shocked at the sight of the pile of dead people they found after the liberation.

Holocaust survivors watch the cart of dead victims that they loaded being taken away.

Monument marking the Jews' struggle
and martyrdom in the Warsaw Ghetto.
The unique monument was made by
Natan Rappaport. He used a stone
called Labradorite which Hitler
ordered in Sweden in 1942 for a
monument to Germany's war victory.

Memorial Museum and Cemetery at
Treblinka—17,000 gravestones.

Wall of memorial plaques in Polish, Yiddish, and Hebrew near Treblinka.

Another memorial located at Majdane.

Symbolic memorial headstone of Dr. Janusz Korcazak who was exterminated at Treblinka.

Jewish Okopowa Cemetery located in Warsaw which includes a memorial grave for the victims of the Nazis.

Warsaw Rabbi Abraham Perlmutter joins a procession to demonstrate his patriotism.

Polish Jews walk the busy crossroads of Al. Jorozolimskie and Ul. Marszalkowska in Warsaw.

Busy shopping street of Warsaw— Ul. Gesia.

Small Polish town where Jews engaged in trade and sold their wares from booths in the town square.

Synagogue in Warsaw which was blown up by Nazis in May 1943.

The Famous Lublin Yeshiva—Jewish School.

Old Synagogue
which is now
being used as
a museum.

Museum of the History and Culture
of the Jews in Krakow—most sacred
building in Poland.

Synagogue at
Bialystock in
Poland.

Nowy Korczyn, Poland—1934

Dov Kupfer (center) and five sons at the Hebrew Day School and Yeshiva.

1936

Jewish Committee of Novy Korczyn, Poland. My father, Dov Kupfer, was a member of this organization. He is located on the bottom row, second person to the left side.

Building in Poland where we hid during the war.

Oldest Synagogue in Poland. Nowy Korczyn.

While Jewish people were being gathered to be transferred to a bigger ghetto, we were hiding in the attic of this home.

Building where my cousin Alan Kupfer and the Raca family hid.

My sister and I are sitting in front with the Mizrachi organization.

Mizrachi organization.

I am operating a lathe machine at school in Landsberg.

ORT's machine shop.

I was the leader of the B'nai Akiba organization.

Leaders of the young people's group.

Picture taken in Poland, 1936. My sister is on the right side with two of our cousins.

Photo of myself taken in Chicago.

My family. Bottom: Samuel Paul and Abie Jack.
Top: Myself, Dov Emil, my wife Rose and Debby Rene.

Sarah and her husband Ichok
Horenfeld on their wedding day.

Sarah and Ichok with their children
Devora and Dov.

With my sister Sarah shortly after our reunion.

High School graduation, Germany.

Winter in Germany.
Harry, Sarah, and I.

Sarah and Harry.

Purim Celebration, 1946.

Hitler's Death Celebration, 1946.

I managed my cousin's store in Chicago.

Mr. and Mrs. Schupach, the family who wanted to adopt me.

Groundbreaking ceremony for the Holocaust Museum. May 20, 1990. El Paso, Texas.

I am giving a speech at the dedication of the Holocaust Museum in El Paso, Texas, in 1992.

I am in front of my family's memorial plaques at the Holocaust Museum.

I was the leader of an organization called Bnei Akiba. I thought even if I couldn't
go to Palestine now, I could help and encourage those who could.

Survivors from my city in Poland. New York, 1956.